ANCHORED

JOYCELIN P. BROWN, B.A., M.A.

WESTBOW
P R E S S®
A DIVISION OF THOMAS NELSON
& ZONDERVAN

WestBow Press books may be ordered through booksellers or by contacting:

WestBow Press
A Division of Thomas Nelson & Zondervan
1663 Liberty Drive
Bloomington, IN 47403
www.westbowpress.com
844-714-3454

Scripture taken from the King James Version of the Bible.

ISBN: 978-1-6642-4096-4 (sc)
ISBN: 978-1-6642-4095-7 (e)

Print information available on the last page.

WestBow Press rev. date: 08/31/2021

CONTENTS

Section B: Intimate Personal Reflections & Thanksgiving

This book of Christian prose and poetry, interspersed with personal anecdotes chronicling my immigrant experience, was inspired through moments of personal devotion and meditation. Presenting it in this format, with much thought and prayer, has truly been a blessing to me, and I sincerely hope you also will be blessed as you read these pages.

Dedicated to my wonderful Husband Trevor Brown, my daughter Trevlin Stewart, my sons Richard and Scott Brown, my grandchildren, Janae Brown-Wright, and Nathaniel and Jonathan Stewart.

Psalm 130:5

I wait for the LORD, my soul doth wait, and in his word do I hope.

Hebrews 6:19

*Which hope we have as an anchor of the
soul, both sure and stedfast, and
which entereth into that within the veil*

ENDORSEMENTS

Rev. Joycelin Brown is a wife and mother who, at the core of her being, is a woman of God with an unwavering passion for helping others pursue and claim their God-ordained destiny. There are many sides to her that might not be readily obvious. She has the incredible capacity to laugh uncontrollably at, or recount a (clean) joke, admonish, encourage, counsel, empathize, intervene in prayer, and find ways to provide material resources wherever she is aware of a need.

This comes as no surprise - it is a reflection of what was instilled in her during her childhood into early adulthood. Her home, 7 Morris Boulevard, was a place where family bonds were sacred. There was a close knit among members of the immediate and extended family. Godly principles were constantly reinforced and modeled. That home not only delighted family and friends, but welcomed countless numbers of individuals who needed shelter, hope, a mother, a word of encouragement. There was always a seat for one more at the table.

The Meditations she shares in this collection are penned with the honesty and candor that I have known her to possess throughout our 40+ years of friendship. The anecdotes drawn from her personal experiences transport the reader into the world of someone who is not concerned with vulnerability. She guides the reader to see how each moment of apparent defeat and hopelessness in her life was canceled and superseded by God's divine provision and purpose. She shares her moments of anxiety when God came through for her and her young family - right on time. She shares truths that forcefully remind us that God will reward, equip, convict, and sometimes surprise those who put their absolute trust in Him. These Meditations are a testament to God's unfathomable ability to do the impossible.

Marian Smile-Senior, M.A.
High School Teacher, U.S.A

The Reverend Joycelin Brown - A Lady of impeccable qualities, who operates and executes with excellence and purpose in any area she is called to task.

As a member of the Pastoral Team at Temple of Praise Church of God, I have known First Lady, Rev. Joycelin Brown, for over a decade. I consider her a mentor and confidant as we interact on both ministerial and social levels. Her pursuit for things concerning the building up of the Kingdom of God is persistent.

She is a Leader in Ministry, an Educator, a Preacher, a Counsellor, and most of all, a humble human being who leads her life with a holistic approach. She is authentic, smart, funny and wise; a woman that is firm but fair in deliberations, and leads with strong Christian principles and beliefs. She is guided by her spiritual and moral compass.

Her deep devotion and spiritual maturity fuel her passion and drive when orchestrating ministerial tasks. Rev. Brown is blessed with many spiritual gifts. She is fruit bearing, and operates in her gifting with divine adequacy. This stalwart organizes and executes many rewarding and uplifting religious and training events, such as: Family, Marital, and Women's Seminars, Information and Teaching Sessions; and Group Facilitations on a variety of topics, especially relevant to youth and women, among many others.

Rev. Brown is a Beacon, not only within the body of Christ, but also in the secular community where she was recognized as an "Unsung Hero" for her work as an Educator. She was also the recipient of the "Lifetime Achievement Award" presented by Rare Diamond Productions for service excellence in education. Her passion for souls of both Christians and non-Christians, propels her into action to respond. Rev. Brown is an advocate for the voiceless. She is resourceful and selfless, which makes her uniquely qualified to respond to calls from fellow citizens.

As a woman of faith, she charts her course marked by the word of God, fueled by prayer, and sustained with thanksgiving.

May the Lord continue to bless Rev. Joycelin Brown in all her life's endeavors. May she soar on Eagles wings.

Rev. Donnett Thompson-Hall,
Award winning International Gospel Recording Artist;
Singer- Songwriter; Ambassador - Compassion Canada

Rev. Joycelin Brown . . .

Every now and again, there comes along a person of a special personage; one who it is difficult to find the right words to describe. Joycelin Brown of Jamaican birth, is one of those persons. A highly trained teacher, Guidance Counsellor and school Administrator, she in her life and career pursued excellence as if her life depended on it. I recall with vivid clarity, the first time I met her, maybe thirty years ago in a seminar, I immediately noted her professional approach, her clarity of perspective on life and on her profession.

No wonder she was able to attain a high level in her profession - High School Administrator. I noticed not only Joycelin's professionalism, and clear perspective on life, but her spiritual perspective. I was privileged to be her Regional Overseer as she completed the Ministerial Credentialing Process with the Church of God: The Ministerial Internship Program, Exhorters' License, and later, Ordained Minister.

I had always hoped that I would have an opportunity to speak on her behalf, because, unfortunately, we articulate how special people are when they are not able to hear.

Unequivocally, Mrs. Joycelin Brown is worthy of our highest accolades, as a person, and certainly, professionally and spiritually.

Dr. Bishop George S. Peart,
Former Regional Overseer of Ontario

Joycelin P. Brown

I first met Mrs. Brown in her grade ten English class over twenty years ago. She quickly transformed from Mrs. Brown, my English teacher, to Mom or Aunty Patsy, my chosen family. Over the years, she has counseled me, encouraged me and included me in her family celebrations.

She coined me as her adopted daughter, I gladly claimed the title, and I am grateful to be a part of the Brown's family. Not only did I gain another Mom, but I gained three additional siblings, who, like their mother, love my son and me unconditionally.

Mrs. Brown was one of few Black teachers I had in my life, even extending onto post-secondary. Before representation was a trending topic, Mrs. Brown was the representation myself and many students needed. Mrs. Brown carries herself with integrity, truth, empathy and love. Her non-judgmental, unconditional love inspired me to be the person I am. Now working in social services with children in foster care, I desire to be a pillar to kids like Mrs. Brown was to me. I want the best for the children with whom I work, as Mrs. Brown wanted for me. Her influence has surpassed her teaching career, as she has been, and continues to be a confidant and a trusted ally to many.

Mrs. Brown is the epitome of a phenomenal woman. She created a safe space for me to bloom as a person, and she taught me to hold my head high and have confidence in myself. Even if we do not speak often, I can always feel her love and her prayers covering me.

Kezia Royer-Burkett, B.A. (Hons).
Past Student

Re: Joycelin Brown

Joycelin Brown is an amazing human being who has secured a special spot in my heart. Her calm spirit, attentiveness and genuine interest in others account for that. It is impossible to associate with her for any period of time without recognizing that this is an authentic individual whose passion is to be God's hand extended to others.

Joycelin is a woman with a big heart. Her capacity to embrace more than just her family, is astonishing. There is a place in her heart for everyone. She is a caring soul whose generosity knows no bounds; a compassionate friend who is able to empathize with the hurting by providing a soft place for them to land in times of turbulence. She is a confidant with whom others can be vulnerable and be sure that the matter is safe.

With confidence in her God-given abilities, Joycelin has impacted the kingdom of God in a significant way. This, however, is without pride and arrogance because she is an authentic portrayal of a servant leader who has dedicated herself to service in the body of Christ.

Joycelin's commitment to the work of the kingdom is making an indelible mark for generations to come. This new contribution, is just another of her efforts to share with others, that which God has deposited in her over the years, so that they may be blessed.

I am delighted to be considered as an integral part of this process, and I am confident that this book, Anchored, will be both inspirational and transformational for countless numbers of persons all over the world.

Wayne A. Vernon, B.Th., M.A.
Lead Pastor,
West Toronto Church of God.

SECTION A

DEVOTION, MEDITATION, POETRY & PERSONAL ANECDOTES

Will your anchor hold in the storms of life,
When the clouds unfold their wings of strife?
When the strong tides lift, and the cables strain,
Will your anchor drift or firm remain?

We have an anchor that keeps the soul
Stedfast and sure while the billows roll,
Fastened to the Rock which cannot move,
Grounded firm and deep in the Savior's love.

A CALL TO GIVE
PRAISES UNTO GOD
(Praise: Exalt, Eulogize, Worship)

Scripture Meditation
Psalms 145; Psalms 150

After living for the past 43 years in Canada, I cannot but reflect on this journey and give praises to Almighty God for having been faithful to my family and me. Migrating to this country in my early twenties; my husband being in his late twenties, life was not always easy. To be honest, being on an International Student visa, having to pay approximately two times the tuition of Canadian students was a huge financial strain. There were times when we found there was absolutely no money to meet our financial needs and we literally had to be helped, frequently by my mom, and occasionally by my husband's dad. Doing odd jobs in Montreal while studying at Concordia University during my first year in Canada taught me to appreciate the little things in life and to praise God for even what I considered small blessings. As soon as we were able to move to Toronto, transferring from Concordia to York University, we did. Toronto would be "greener pastures", I thought. As I look back and think of how faithful God has been to us, I thank and praise Him for having put us on this journey, one on which He never left us alone. Coming from a situation where literally everything was provided for me, considering ourselves as "middle class" in our country, and coming to Toronto where we literally had nothing, we learnt some very humbling life lessons. I understand now that sometimes God has to break us so that He can mould us into what He wants us to be. With absolutely no family in Toronto, God placed great friends in our lives (many you will read about later in this book). We have remained friends to this day. I pause to praise God for all that he has done in our lives and the role he allowed our friends to play.

Every day I will extol the name of the Lord. No day shall pass without me praising God, thanking him for His many blessings and gifts. We should cultivate a continuous atmosphere of praise so that we will praise God when we "feel like", and even when we "don't feel like".

Writers of the Old Testament used various words to call upon the Israelites to Praise God. These are most times used interchangeably in the Psalms. Three such words are:-
Barak . . . to bless God in an act of adoration (Ps. 95:6)
Halal . . . (from which comes "Hallelujah" - often referred to as the highest praise) means "Praise the Lord"
(Ps. 149:3)
Yadah . . . sometimes translated "Give thanks" (Ps. 63:1).

Psalms 145:8 reminds us that, *the LORD is gracious, and full of compassion; slow to anger, and of great mercy.* This expresses God's delight in showing mercy. When God sees misery, he is moved by compassion and mercy towards us. There are times when our soul is in distress, and totally burdened down, but even then we must remember to praise God. It is through our praise that we experience his compassion.

David who wrote the Psalms had many things for which to praise God. He had victory over Goliath; he was saved many times from Saul's jealous pursuits; and he experienced many victories in battles; understandingly though, he did not only praise God in the good times. I imagine he also did in the bad times when he felt forsaken by God and asked his soul, *why are thou cast down within me,* but he encouraged his soul to, *hope thou in God* (Ps. 42:5).

There are times like David, when we will feel like we are in the lowest depth of the pit, but David reminds us about the power of offering praise to God. David says, *while I live will I praise the LORD: I will sing praises unto my God while I have any being* (Ps. 146:2). That should be the prayer of every individual today and always.

Every worship service, every individual worship, every home and every person should be filled with praise for God. Psalms 147:5-7 states, *Great is our Lord, and of great power: his understanding is infinite*, thus we should *sing unto the LORD with thanksgiving; sing praise upon the harp unto our God.*

It is often said that if man refuses to praise God, He will allow nature to do so; thus, David calls upon nature to Praise God; *Praise ye him, sun and moon: praise him, all ye stars of light. Praise him, you heavens of heavens, and you waters that be above the heavens . . . creeping things, and flying fowl* (Ps. 148: 3-10). And in vs. 11-14, he reminds us that all mankind should continually give praise to God, *Kings of the earth, and all people; princes, and all judges of the earth: Both young men, and maidens; old men, and children.*

Psalms 150, reiterates the importance of praising God. *Praise God in his sanctuary: praise him in the firmament of his power. . . **Let everything that hath breath praise the LORD. Praise ye the LORD.***

When we meditate on all that God has done in creation and redemption and in our personal lives, we can and should lift up our voices in praise to Him. Praise then becomes a POWERFUL RESPONSE of the heart, expressing joy, gratitude and a desire to communicate with God. In addition to praising with our voices in the sanctuary, we can praise him with living our lives with love and joy, with devotion to His word and with the proclamation of the Gospel.

Praising God MUST be a lifestyle for the Christians. He inhabits our praise. Praises go up and the blessings come down. Praise the clouds away. Praise him through dark situations. Praise Him in the good and the bad times. *I will praise thee, O LORD, with my whole heart; I will shew forth all thy marvellous works* (Ps. 9:1).

GOD'S GLORY

Scripture Meditation
Ezekiel 10

The term "Glory of God" is used several ways in the scriptures. It sometimes describes God's splendour and majesty; *Thine, O LORD is the greatness, and the power, and the glory, and the victory, and the majesty: for all that is in the heaven and in the earth is thine; thine is the kingdom, O LORD, and thou art exalted as head above all* (1 Chr. 29:11).

In Ezekiel 1:26-28, The Glory of God designates His uniqueness, His holiness and His transcendence. The glory of God also refers to God's visible presence among His people, referred to by Rabbis as the Shekinah glory, meaning the dwelling of God; used to describe the visible manifestation of God's presence and glory. There are many illustrations of this in scripture: Moses saw God's glory in the pillar of cloud and fire (Ex. 13:21); God's glory covered Mount Sinai when God gave Moses the law (Ex. 24:16-17); God's glory filled Solomon's temple (1 Kgs. 8:11); and Stephen saw the glory of Jesus at the time of his martyrdom (Acts 7:55), just to mention a few.

The New Testament equivalent of the Shekinah glory is Jesus Christ himself, who, as the glory of God, came to make His dwelling among humans, *And the Word was made flesh, and dwelt among us, (and we beheld his glory, the glory as of the only begotten of the Father,) full of grace and truth* (John 1:14)

Another element of God's glory is His (felt) presence and power. *The heavens declare the glory of God; and the firmament sheweth his handywork* (Ps. 19:1) and, *one cried unto another, and said, Holy, holy, holy, is the* LORD *of hosts: the whole earth is full of his glory* (Is. 6:3).

Believers experience God's glory in His nearness, in His love, in His righteousness and in His manifestation through the power of the Holy Spirit, *But we all, with open face beholding as in a glass the glory of the Lord, are changed into the same image from glory to glory, even as by the Spirit of the Lord* Spirit (II Cor. 3:18).

The overarching questions I would pose to believers today is: Is God's glory manifesting in your life? Are you experiencing his love? Are you living in holiness and righteousness so that His glory can be manifested in your life?

It is important to note that any kind of sin will prevent the glory of God from manifesting in one's life. When God manifests His glory in a person's life, God's name must be glorified. Everything that person does must be done, not for self-gratification or vain glory, but must bring glory to God.

Paul calls Jesus *the Lord of Glory* (1 Cor. 2:8). James calls Him, *our Lord Jesus Christ, the Lord of glory* (Jas. 2:1). The miracles of Jesus and the life he lived reveal the glory of God. In like manner, the Christian's life must reveal the glory of God. Is your walk revealing His glory? Is your talk revealing His glory? Are your conversations revealing His glory? When we engage in evil conversation against our brothers and sisters, are we revealing God's glory?

Our daily lives should welcome the glory of God. Let us live in the spirit so that we can always entertain the glory of God and experience His awesome presence in our lives. Believers like you and I who are redeemed by the blood have the spirit of glory resting on us (I Pet. 4:14). This is an awesome feeling of confidence when we live in God's glory!

Let us not allow the glory of God to depart from us. In Ezekiel chapter 10, the glory of the Lord departed from the people because of their idolatry and unrepentance before God. God left the Temple reluctantly and gradually. If we permit sin and worldliness to gain place in our hearts, then God's glory and presence will depart. He is a holy God and cannot dwell where sin abides.

Is God's glory able to remain in your temple today or is He gradually leaving?

Let us examine ourselves – thoughts, and deeds and see if God's glory can reside in our temple. We must passionately desire God's glory and presence as we seek to fervently hate sin and immorality. We will experience God's glory when we walk in righteousness, holiness and obedience to Him, allowing the spirit to be fully active in our walk (1 Pet. 4:14). As believers, our ultimate glory will be experienced when we come face to face with our Maker!

NEW BEGINNINGS –
IN HIS STRENGTH ALONE

Scripture Meditation
Zechariah 4:6

*Then he answered and spake unto me, saying, this
is the word of the LORD unto Zerubbabel, saying,
Not by might, nor by power, but by my
spirit, saith the LORD of hosts.*

*We had worshipped at a church in the city of Toronto for 20 years,
our first place of worship after we landed here. Every now and then
my husband and I reminisce on the beautiful fellowship that existed
in that congregation. Everyone loved each other, everyone looked out
for each other and we shared everything among each other. It was a
true representation of the early church in Acts where everyone had
things in common. We had served the Lord in various capacities in
that church. My husband had served on the Pastor's Council for many
years and was still serving. I had been Youth Leader, District Youth
Director, Sunday School Superintendent, you name it. Despite all that,
however, there was one thing that became so strong that to continue
worshipping there would jeopardize our continued walk with God.
Every Sunday we would literally leave church murmuring about what
one particular person of importance had done; we were becoming
murmuring Christians. We loved the people but we soon realized
after much prayer and seeking the Lord, that in order for us to survive
as Christians we had to make a move. With much anxiety, we spoke
with the Pastor, Pastor Andy, a kind, dear friend, and expressed to
him that we were now ready to worship at another church. This was*

a new beginning which we embarked on with much trepidation. We were uprooting our family and leaving the comfort of our church home after having served there for 20 years! Our children resented the move. At home, we had many fights about it. We were scared that they would become resentful. God knew, however, that we needed this new beginning and He prepared the way for us. He allowed our new pastor and wife Bishop and Lady C. Hall, and the new congregation to welcome us with open arms. The Pastor and his wife saw that we were hurting and they bound our wounds which were deep, and led us on a path to a new relationship with our God. New beginnings are sometimes scary, but with God everything is very possible.

It is remarkable how many people leave a New Year's Night Service proclaiming that they are going to be "better this year". As a child and youth, I remember going to the altar at every New Year's Eve service. I would earnestly pray that God would forgive me of all my transgression, "wipe the slate clean" (that was the expression then; we had no computers, we couldn't use terms like "delete"). I would rise from the altar feeling fully purged and ready to serve God. I was determined that in that new year I would read my bible every day, I would pray 3 times per day and I would, I would, I would. These were good intentions which lasted for the first week, maybe a month, but as the year progressed, I slowly drifted back into my old habits.

As I struggled with my desire to do right, I soon realized it is not by my strength but by the strength that God gives that we are able to remain constant in our pursuit for holiness. God calls upon us to live holy 365 days per year, not just the first day or the first month of every year.

Holiness should be our lifestyle; it should be natural as we walk in God's presence, led by His spirit. Struggles of life may deter us from the path at times, but God expects that His children will be renewed daily and be willing to walk uprightly every day.

We are not able to make this happen by ourselves, but through the Spirit of God that dwells within our hearts. It is that same Spirit who has come to *reprove the world of sin, and of righteousness, and of judgment* (John 16:8). Our total dependency should be on the Holy Spirit to daily create "new beginnings" in our hearts. Let us give God a chance on the first day of the year and every other day, to create in us a clean heart and continually guide us in the path of righteousness.

As a youth we sang the song, *If you have tried everything and everything failed . . . turn it over to Jesus and you can smile the rest of your days.* The cited scripture passage reminds us that like Zerubbabel, our strength is not in our might and our prowess. Our strength comes totally from God. Every decision we make in life should be anchored in God.

Have you been struggling to do it on your own? Have you been feeling totally defeated after each effort? Are you at a crossroads today where you are struggling with making a new decision? Be reminded, we are only victorious when we totally commit our ways to God. *Commit thy way unto the Lord; trust also in him; and he shall bring it to pass* (Ps. 35:5). Let us bask in the all-powerful strength of our Almighty God. There is complete confidence in His ability to keep us on the path of righteousness. Many have failed trying to do it on their own, many others will fail repeating that same path, but those who trust in God shall "be like Mount Zion". Be encouraged. In His strength you are well able to move forward into new beginnings.

My Pastor's Wife

She strides with elegance in her steps
A familiar hello, a quiet bow, a pleasant "good day" to all
Quiet at times, verbal at others, with words
fitly spoken, and sometimes not!
She is human! And errs as such
She is our Pastor's wife

But, she is more than that!
A kind example to all,
Set apart with utmost honour.
Words of wisdom from her lips exude
Providing joyous comfort for friends and family alike
Perpetual love emanates for husband and children

Her Children rise up and call her blessed
Her grace and poise surpass her circumstances
Amidst life's struggles, Amidst life's pains
Amidst its joy and boundless blessings
With radiant joy she lives on
With hope of loved-ones to behold!

She is our Pastor's wife!
She is a virtuous woman!
A Woman of great strength!
She is a Woman of God!

INTIMATE RELATIONSHIP
WITH GOD # I

True Acquaintance

Scripture Meditation
Job 22:21-30

Coming from Montreal to Toronto with no other family member in this city, things were "tough". In the church we attended, a young couple who will be named Charm and Zeke befriended us. They were our angels sent from God. They instantly built an acquaintance with us. We immediately felt secure in their friendship and we trusted them. Every Sunday they took us back and forth to church. Readers, you might not know what the Canadian winters of the 70s and 80s were like, but they were brutal. What a joy it was to know we had a ride to and from church every Sunday. It was most uplifting to know that we had built acquaintance with this lovely couple and we could rely on their friendship. A famous Jamaican saying goes, "A friend in need is a friend in deed!" Indeed these two young people quickly grew from being mere acquaintances to becoming our trusted friends.

Job's three friends are known to us in modern times as miserable comforters, mostly because of the advice they gave him in his time of sickness.

The words of Eliphaz, reflected his wrong concepts and his erroneous theology of suffering. A big question for modern day readers is, *Were Job's friend's assertions truly wrong?* On close reading of the story of Job, however, we will conclude that their simple notion of suffering and their assertions against Job were incorrect. By the end of the book of Job they would see the flawed ideologies in their beliefs.

They literally accused Job of sinning, thus his illness. Regardless, Eliphaz's words contained some profound truths as they related to having an acquaintance with God. He pointed out what he thought Job had done to sin against God (Job 22: 1-20). Though he was wrong about Job, he said some truths about God.

Eliphaz made a final appeal for Job to return to God, to *Acquaint now thyself with him, and be at peace: thereby good shall come unto thee.* (Job 22:21). Markedly, Eliphaz believed that there was a great lack in Job's life.

Our new acquaintances referred to in the anecdote got to know us and we got to know them, and soon we were comfortable in their presence and in sharing with them. The first step to be at peace with God is "getting to know" Him in a personal way. It requires an acquaintance; having a personal intimacy with God through reading, studying and meditating on His word. It also requires being in constant communication with Him through prayer

In the garden, Adam lost his intimacy and acquaintance with God and was separated from Him; *And I will put enmity between thee and the woman, and between thy seed and her seed; it shall bruise thy head, and thou shalt bruise his heel* (Gen. 3:15). Divine friendship, therefore, had to be set up on a different basis. Sin implies separation from, and enmity with God. Intimacy is destroyed through sin. Acquaintance implies reunion and peace with God. No man can be acquainted with God and be a stranger to Jesus, as Jesus bears the combined image of God and man. It is clear then, that our full acquaintance with God is contingent on our relationship with Jesus Christ His son.

In order to have ultimate fellowship with God we need more than a chance encounter with the Lord our Saviour. We need an intimate acquaintance with Him.

If you have strayed from your intimate relationship with God, there comes a time in your life when you need to find your way back into favour with Him. The path back into fellowship with God is very simple and easy to the willing heart. Job 22:22 & 23 give two important words: **Receive** . . . *Receive, I pray thee, the law from his mouth, and lay up his words in thine heart.* . . and **Return.** *If thou return to the Almighty, thou shalt be built up.* We are all called upon to receive the word of truth in our hearts and return to our maker.

The good news is, we can return just as we are, *weary, broken, discouraged, and disappointed, and* He is right there to receive us, and to build not just a mere acquaintance, but a solid relationship with us.

Being God's Friend

Staying close to him in intimate relationship
Talking to him "face to face" as Moses did
As His friend - totally devoted to him.
Half of me - just not enough.

Giving one hundred percent is a MUST!
The only way to go!
As my friend, close communion share
Sharing my joys, my sorrows, my pains
My good days and the bad ones too
Always seeking to know His ways . . .
Growing daily in this profound union
Growing in purpose, so that I, indeed become God's friend!

Seeking for His heart, His purpose, His wisdom,
Yes! His holy principles and even remembering His sufferings

O God!
Knowing you more
Becoming a better friend
Finding grace in your sight.
Finding daily favors just calling your name
Knowing your voice and obeying same
Standing on words and precepts truly Holy

Loyalty in friendship I pray – my loyalty
Yours is sure!
Be my strength dear Lord
And my faith in moments of weakness
Be near me always.
Be my source O Lord. Be my friend.

INTIMATE RELATIONSHIP WITH GOD # II

Rebuilding Acquaintance

Scripture Meditation
Isaiah 55:1

*Ho, every one that thirsteth, come ye to the
waters, and he that hath no money; come
ye, buy, and eat; yea, come, buy wine and
milk without money and without price.*

As we were being counseled before marriage by my husband's late
father, Bishop James Brown, I can still vividly remember him telling
us that "only two fools" live together over an extended period of time
and never quarreled. He cautioned, however, that it was the making
up that was the most important part of that experience. Years after,
as my husband and I journeyed in our marriage we began to fully
understand the magnitude of that counsel. There were times when we
had big quarrels, huge ones! Lord this must be the end of our marriage!
This relationship is coming to an end! The sky is falling! There were
times, I am sure Trev didn't want to see me, and to be perfectly truthful,
I didn't want to see him either. But the words of his late father always
rang in my ears, "It's the making up" that matters. And believe me,
though during the heat of those quarrels I felt like Trev didn't like me
much, and at times that I didn't want the relationship; I must confess,
some of the most wonderful, exhilarating times we have had in our
marriage are those "making up" moments! We soon found out, it

wasn't so much about the fight, it was more about the reconciling and rebuilding of our relationship.

It is time to rebuild the intimate relationship you and I once had with Christ; time to begin to read our bibles again; begin to pray again, time to seek Him on our faces like we did before. It is time to groan in earnestness before Him and rebuild our acquaintance with the Living God. God calls out to mankind for relationship. He gives an invitation to the thirsty, *Ho, every one that thirsteth, come ye to the waters, and he that hath no money; come ye, buy, and eat; yea, come, buy wine and milk without money and without price* (Isa. 55:1)

Once we start to build a relationship with Christ, He has a way of renewing our nature. Job 22:23 reminds us that if we return to God, we *"shalt be built up"*. God is willing and ready to rebuild what the cankerworm has stolen from us: spiritual joy, our peace, our ability and desire to read the word and commune with God; and anything else that the devil has stolen. *We are his workmanship, created in Christ Jesus unto good works, which God hath before ordained that we should walk in them* (Eph. 2:10).

Truly God is able to build us up by creating or recreating a new and dynamic relationship with us. If you have a spouse, consider the biggest fights that you have had in marriage, like the fights I mentioned between my husband and me earlier. If there is no spouse, think of this in light of your siblings, parents or any other cherished relationship. Think of how empty you felt when you were out of sync in this relationship. Then think of the makeup; the day or night, and the overflowing joy you experienced. Place these thoughts into any important relationship in your life. Then multiply the joy many times, and that is what we experience when we return to God in body, soul and spirit!

When we fall on our knees in penitence before God, our acquaintance with Him can again become one of intimacy. He is able to shape us and mold us into the creatures He wants us to become. I have often sung the song, *"Have Thine Own Way Lord, Have Thine Own Way"*, then we go on to ask him to "break" us and "mould" us and "make" us after His will. We must make ourselves malleable in this acquaintance. We understand that we are the clay and He becomes the potter. *"But now, O LORD, thou art our father; we are the clay, and thou our potter; and we all are the work of thy hand"* (Isa. 64:8). It is when we bare before the Lord in this manner that He is able to build the relationship that He wants with us and we become intimately acquainted with Him.

SUBSTITUTIONARY ATONEMENT

Scripture Meditation
Psalms 32:1-2
Blessed is he whose transgression is
forgiven, whose sin is covered.
Blessed is the man unto whom the Lord imputeth
not iniquity, and in whose spirit there is no guile.

Christ's death on the cross and his resurrection three days later is central to the Christian faith, and the forgiveness of our sins. Through this eternal event, He pardons us from all our sins and ill-deeds. Just think of it – no matter how wild or vile a sinner one was, His advent to the Cross and His resurrection has given that one freedom from sin and death!

Our sins are covered and our evil past is put out of sight, once we come to him in penitence! He takes away the imputation of our sins; the guilt is cancelled from our record! Amazing!
We have not earned His forgiveness, but through His grace we receive it as a gift – the gift of forgiveness!

As we follow Christ, we model the prayer He laid out for us. As we ask Him to forgive us of our sins, to cover and not impute, we also forgive our debtors and people who trespass against us.

For many people, it is sometimes easier to *say* than to *do*; and that is where we struggle. It is not necessarily because we do not want to forgive, but being humans, we hurt, and when we experience hurt from others, our "humanness" makes it difficult to forget the pain and hurt. It is understandable then, that we at times find it difficult to forgive. In our own strength it is impossible to do it. Thus, we pray daily for the courage; because it does take courage, to forgive, to cover or put out of sight the real or perceived injustice or hurt that we have experienced.

Yes, it can be hard to forgive, or not impute the transgression of others; and sometimes it takes a longer time than at other times. We, however, MUST forgive in order to heal and move forward. If we try to get answers for everything and every situation we will not be able to forgive the "sins" that others commit against us. The only thing we see in our struggles and strivings to get the answers is the hurt that they have caused us, and then we hurt more, and it dawdles longer.

Let us see our forgiveness in the light of Christ's substitutionary death on our behalf. We went against God's laws. We did everything that we should not have done! Yet, in God's infinite mercy He sent His only son to be the substitute for us, to die in our stead so that we can be called "Children of God", and live! *For God so loved the world that he gave His only begotten son that who so ever believeth on Him should not perish but have everlasting life* (John 3:16).

Just think of it – His substitution for us means we do not have to die in sin! He forgave us, Let us now forgive others!

BEING FILLED WITH THE SPIRIT

Scripture Meditation
Ephesians 5:11-21

Being filled with the spirit in this context refers to the constant and continuous renewal of the Holy Spirit that believers need in our Christian walk. This filling enables us to resist evil and to speak out against evil in our homes, church, and community at large. It is the empowering force that allows us to stand up minutely, hourly and daily for Christ. This filling is needed for worship, for witness, and for maintaining a lifestyle that is worthy of God's presence in our lives. We must fully yield minute by minute to the leading of the Holy Spirit.

As we are continuously "walking in the Spirit" we experience continuous infilling as the Holy Spirit provides the push that moves the believer along the path of complete obedience to God and His word. Being filled with the spirit means that a believer is not motivated by his own desire or his own will to succeed, but is fully motivated by God and his obedience to do what God wills; thus walking always in the path that God chooses for him.

We are admonished to yield to the total control of the Holy Spirit; so every passion, thought, and deed is under His direction. The cited passage reminds us that being filled with the spirit means being filled with the word, being in constant prayer, serving others, having holy desires, giving thanks in psalms and hymns, submitting to one another. Colossians 3:16 parallels verse 19 of the cited text, as it reminds us to, *Let the word of Christ dwell in you richly in all wisdom;*

teaching and admonishing one another in psalms and hymns and spiritual songs, singing with grace in your hearts to the Lord.

Paul intimates here that the believer can be filled with the Spirit only when he is controlled by the Word.

This means that we know the truth and obey it. Hymns and spiritual songs are languages of the heart that bring us closer to God and help to maintain our daily filling. They are ways of expressing our overflowing joy in worship to God. He deserves this worship.

Being filled with the spirit means that we have to be mindful of, and refrain from evil associations; *And have no fellowship with the unfruitful works of darkness, but rather reprove them* (Eph. 5: 11). We must model good deeds, and similarly, cry out against unrighteousness. We should never turn a blind eye to sin. That can become dangerous for our spiritual life and is detrimental to our yearning desire to be filled with the Spirit. We are reminded very forcefully in Ephesians 5 to be *filled with the spirit*, then we will be able to speak, *to yourselves in psalms and hymns and spiritual songs, singing and making melody in your heart to the Lord* (Eph5: 18-19). This brings to us the daily renewal of the Spirit that we need to sustain us. The believer needs to be filled for worship, for service and for witness, maintaining a "living" relationship with Christ.

May our prayer today be that we entertain the presence of the Holy Spirit in our lives, every moment of the day!

A PERSONAL DECISION

Scripture Meditation
Genesis 18:19
*For I know him, that he will command his
children and his household after him, and they
shall keep the way of the Lord, to do justice
and judgment; that the Lord may bring upon
Abraham that which he hath spoken of him.*

*I asked my husband, "Can we go out to dinner tonight?" His response,
"The money we are going to use to do that could buy us dinner for a
week". No, he was not stingy, far from it. He was just the practical
one in our relationship. He knew we didn't have much money and he
wanted to spend it wisely. That was wisdom, but I wanted an evening
out! We just couldn't afford it. . . A reasonable decision. Many years
later we laughed at that. As newlyweds and in a new country, we made
a decision to place God at the centre of our lives; and though we had
many challenges, God remained faithful to us. Presently, we could go
out to dinner every evening of the week, if we so desired! This is not
boasting. It is following the principle my grandmother taught me,
"Take care of God's business and He will take care of yours". He has
certainly done that!*

In life we are constantly faced with decisions. Depending on the
circumstance, we rely on various things and people to help us make
these decisions. We ask our friends or family for their opinion; we
weigh the pros and cons of these decision we will make; then after
careful consideration, we decide one way or the other. When it comes
to decisions about worldly or material things, though it may be costly,
we can afford to make mistakes at times. There is one decision,

however, about which we cannot make a mistake. (It is not as simple as deciding whether we go out for dinner or not). It determines if we live or die; and determines where we spend eternity.

As we make this important decision there are certain things that we need to consider:

a). **Determination** - each person must purpose in his or her heart on the way he or she must take, and must be determined with God's help to take the path that leads to life. If God sees our focus, He will honour our determination. *For I know him, that he will command his children and his household after him, and they shall keep the way of the LORD, to do justice and judgment; that the LORD may bring upon Abraham that which he hath spoken of him* (Gen.18:19).

b) **Reflection** - In order to make personal decisions we sometimes need to reflect on the past. I think of the familiar song, "Remind me dear Lord. Show me where you brought me from and where I could have been".

When we are faced with situations and are tempted to make the wrong decisions, we need to ask God to remind us. Do you remember when you wanted . . .? Do you remember when you promised God that . . .?

Then when we reflect on how God brought us through, we will be more determined in our hearts to make a decision to follow His leading.

Reflection allows us to see that the Lord has done "great" and "marvelous" things for us. *Then was our mouth filled with laughter, and our tongue with singing: then said they among the heathen, The LORD hath done great things for them* (Ps. 126:2). *For he that is mighty hath done to me great things; and holy is his name* (Luke 1:49).

When we reflect on all the great things that He has done in our lives we cannot help but serve Him. There are times when we are not at our best. We falter and we fail. We become frail. But just a reflection of God's greatness gets us excited and ready to follow.

It is easy to make decisions to follow Christ when everything is going well. It is when the contrary winds are blowing that it becomes more difficult to decide to remain in the "ship". We must, however, make a serious declaration to stay on board. When I was a child, Christians used to testify "Comes what may . . .
But those same Christian when the difficulties came were nowhere to be seen. My grandmother used to say, "Dem say comes what may but when may comes you no see dem" (translation: "They'll say comes what may, but when things get rough they are nowhere to be found")

The depth of our determination is tested when we are faced with trials. That is when we need a serious declaration to stand, and when we need to ask God to help us make a decisive stand. We need to remind ourselves that we are witnesses of what Christ has done. We must be strong and courageous witnesses.

When we make the decision to follow the Lord, we pledge to follow him in righteousness and holiness. We desire to study His word so that we will grow and mature in Him *(I Pet. 2:2)*. We make a decision to put away the things of the *old man (Eph. 4:22)*, and to put on the things of the *new man (Eph. 4:24)*. We make a decision to serve him regardless *(Rom. 8:35)*.

We also make a decision to bear fruit for His Kingdom *(John 15:2-8)* and to live a consecrated life before God *(I Cor. 6:11)*. We must make the decision to serve him sacrificially. It **must** cost us something.

Let us be resolute in our decision to follow Christ. Let us reflect on all that He has done and all that He has been to us. Our decision to follow and live for Him is not based on what our friends or family members will say or do. It is not contingent on circumstances. It is despite circumstances; I am persuaded and I am committed.

BE STRONG IN THE LORD -
PUT ON THE ARMOUR OF GOD

Scripture Meditation
Ephesians 6:10-18

Finally, my brethren, be strong in the Lord, and in the power of his might (Eph. 6:10). Being strong in the Lord means that we, through His grace and power are able to withstand the wiles of the devil; to withstand the *principalities* and *powers and rulers of darkness of this world* (Eph. 6:12). That is not an easy task and most certainly cannot be accomplished on our own. The scripture reminds us of things we need to do to be strong in the Lord.

We must have our *loins girt with truth*. In secular warfare, before engaging in combat, soldiers would provide themselves maximum freedom of movement for their legs by tucking their tunic in their belts. So it is in the spiritual warfare. We are called upon to have our "loins girt about". This means that we, like the soldier must be prepared at all times. This is the only way we can withstand the wiles of the enemy.
We must wear and be totally shielded with the *breastplate of righteousness*; or we will be attacked and defeated.

Our feet must be *shod with the preparation of the gospel of peace*. Many run with swift feet to make mischief. As Christians, when we run, it is with the "gospel of peace". We should also continually wear the *shield of faith*. In war the shield is used as a defensive tool. When the darts come at the soldier he is able to fight them off using his shield. As Christians, fiery darts come at us daily. If we are protected by *the shield of faith* we are less likely to be hurt.

Not only do we need our shield but we must be guarded *with the helmet of salvation.* The devil aims for our heads. He knows that if he can confuse us and allow us to question God's existence and his omnipotence, he has us vulnerable to his whims. Thus we must ensure that the "helmet of salvation" is securely fixed and we have fully clothed ourselves with the full armor; thus we are able to stand firm.

In this warfare, our biggest weapon is the *sword of the spirit – God's word.* We must read it daily, feed on it, meditate on it, live by it, and love it with our life! That is an absolute must if we are to survive on this battlefield. Our daily tasks must be prayer and supplication in the spirit. We must open our mouths boldly to proclaim the gospel of Jesus Christ and to claim victory in Him and through Him. There are situations that will attempt to rob us of our praise and our faith in His ability to be ALL. Be aware of those situations! Keep covered with the helmet. Guard your mind and soul against them. God must always remain the source of our strength. Be strong in the Lord and in the power of HIS might!

Called Upon

Called upon to stand – regardless
Upon the rock
Upon a mountain
Called upon to swim the ocean that leads to Him

Who has called?
God has
Stand firm, be unmovable, abounding always
Search the good Book
As horizons expand
Deeper depths- higher heights
Live, Learn and Grow

Called upon to beat the odds
Called upon to shine through the dark
Called upon to be a tower of strength
Called upon to be a candlestick

Who has called?
God has
So, you can do all things through His strength
Shine in a world embodied with darkness
You are a lighthouse –
Called upon to Shine
Called upon to Be!

GOD'S PROVIDENTIAL CARE # I

Leaving the Past Behind Following His Direction

Scripture Meditation
Exodus 14

After I completed my first degree at York University I went to business places all over the city to find jobs. Upon receiving my resume, I would get the call for an interview, but once I entered the office, I would be told the job was taken. Needless to say, on a few occasions, I would go back on the street, make an inquiry about the job from a pay phone (no cell phone then) and surprise, surprise, the job was still open. On one occasion I was told I was "too qualified" for a hotel front desk job, and they would be wasting their time to train me as I would leave if I got a better job; but in the same breath I was offered a housekeeping job in that same establishment! Discouraged, I just wanted to pack my things and return to Jamaica. I had got the degree I came for. My husband was getting pretty low in spirit too. Nothing seemed to be working. There were times when we wondered if God cared and if staying in Canada was in His will for us.

Eventually, I wrote something very desperate on a major banking institution job application form. The moment I returned home the phone rang. It was the bank. The person's statement to me was, "You seem very angry with the system". I responded, "Yes I am totally frustrated, as everyone is telling me I need "Canadian" experience but no one will give me a chance to earn it. Her response, "When are you able to come in for an interview"? I went the next day, a Thursday, and started working the following Monday. Then within a month the Ontario Ministry of Education (No Ontario College of Teachers then) assessed my credentials for teaching in Ontario and decided I needed to do a course to supplement my Teacher Education Completed in Jamaica. Wow! How could I leave the job that I had worked so hard to get, to return to school? God had it all mapped out! Before the course at the University of Toronto started, I applied for and got an evening job within the same institution; so I was able to complete my course in the day. What a mighty God we serve! He knows just the path He has mapped out for us; if we only allow Him to lead as we follow, He will certainly care for us.

Throughout the first 13 chapters of Exodus, there are some prominent themes and occurrences; most of which represent the degraded conditions of the Israelite:

- Cry of the Israelites to God regarding their task masters
- God's call to Moses to go to Egypt
- Pharaoh's hard heart
- Plagues: frogs, lice, flies, death of cattle, boils, hail and fire, locusts, darkness
- God's final plague – death of the first born
- Feast of unleavened bread - cleansing
- God's people being set free
- Exodus (departure) from Egypt

In Chapter 13:19 we are told, *"And Moses took the bones of Joseph with him: for he had straitly sworn the children of Israel, saying, God will surely visit you; and ye shall carry up my bones away hence with you.* To the Israelite, Egypt represented BONDAGE, OPPRESSION, and SLAVERY. Joseph did not want his bones left in Egypt. As Christians, when God takes us out of a terrible situation, we should not look back. We must purpose in our hearts to go forward with all earnestness. When we do that, we will experience God's providential care.

We must be fervent in our hearts to put the oppression of the past behind and go forward with God. Nothing good is left in "Egypt" for the believer, and when we yearn to go back we yearn to return to slavery. In my anecdote, God opened doors for me though the circumstances looked dismal at first, but once the door opened, I never looked back. I followed where God was leading. We must free ourselves of the physical, emotional and mental slavery of the past. "Egypt" in the believer's life is synonymous with the stronghold sin had on us in our past life. This includes, but not limited to defeats we experienced, and the sadness and difficulties of our past. We must be determined in our hearts, never to go back to "Egypt". There is a better land ahead. We must follow God's direction as He leads us to the "Promise Land".

God's providential care is always eminent when we allow Him to lead. *And the LORD went before them by day in a pillar of a cloud, to lead them the way; and by night in a pillar of fire, to give them light; to go by day and night* (Ex. 13:21).

When God goes before us, we have nothing to fear, we are fully protected; no harm can befall us.
Yea, though I walk through the valley of the shadow of death, I will fear no evil: for thou art with me; thy rod and thy staff they comfort me (Ps. 23:4)

GOD'S PROVIDENTIAL CARE # II

He will Fight for You

Scripture Meditation
Exodus 14

In Exodus Chapter 14, God's Providential Care is manifested. In Vv. 1 & 2 the LORD spoke to Moses, giving specific direction as to the route the Israelites must go. It behooves us to follow God's instructions if we want to stay under His care. God always goes ahead and prepares the way. He knew Pharaoh's heart. God always knows the heart of the enemy, and knows the enemy is always in full pursuit of God's children.

Pharaoh thought the Israelites would be ensnared in the wilderness. What he did not know, was that God had the ability to free His people from every entanglement. When God's people follow His instructions - they confound the enemy. When the enemy expects failure, God says no. There is no failure in God. There is no entanglement in the wilderness. As a youth and into adulthood, a song we used to sing is "*So let the storm rage high, they don't worry me for I am sheltered safe within the arms of God. He walks with me and naught of earth can harm me for I am sheltered safe within the arms of God*. Sometimes we tend to forget those words, no matter how often we sing them. When pursued, we grumble and complain.

In vs. 10-12 (cited text), as the people approached the red sea, Pharaoh drew near and the people became fearful and contentious.

They chided Moses for bringing them to die in the wilderness. They immediately forgot the signs they had seen in Egypt, wrought by God through Moses.

How often do we forget His ability to care for us! These were the same people who had been in bondage and whom God had delivered. God had heard their cries of oppression and had come through for them. These were the same people who were now doubting God.

Alas! Let us not be quick to criticize them and call them murmuring folks; as many times we find ourselves in very similar situations, forgetting God's providential care of the past and not acknowledging that He is still able to deliver us through any situation; thus we murmur and complain. How easily we forget!!!!

In times of stress we "want" to go back to "Egypt", to the sinful path from which we were freed. We easily forget the oppression of the past. Let us not go back to the brick and hard life, the boils and the sores. Let us remain in God's providential care.

Remain confident in the God you serve and allow Him to lead your path. Amidst the battles you face: financial, physical, emotional, spiritual; amidst frustration and discouragement, God's providential care is always extended to you.

Fear not, stand still, and see what God will do. He will destroy your enemies, *the Egyptians*, and you will see them again, no more. *"The Lord shall fight for you, and you shall hold your peace* (Ex. 14:14)!

GOD'S PROVIDENTIAL CARE # III

Going Forward

Scripture Meditation:
Exodus 14

My sister friend and her husband Charm and Zeke mentioned earlier, greatly impacted our lives. The husband was the person who gave Trev the money to buy a pair of safety shoes for his first job in Toronto. His wife was the one who planned and executed by first baby shower. I knew no one in Toronto and I had come from Montreal pregnant with our first child. She was the one I called when my husband had gone to work early in the morning and I went into labour. She was at my house within minutes, calling a taxi to take me to the hospital. Needless to say she has told stories of how I screamed at her throughout the day, during the agony of labour pain. She was the first person to see our daughter. My husband was still making his way on bus, to the hospital when she was born. This sister-friend was also the one who saw me crying the next day and instinctively offered to babysit for me, knowing that I had to return to University a week after I had given birth. It didn't end there. When I cried from the bus into her apartment at Stong Court in Toronto, (because it was so cold and I had to take 3 buses to her home with a 3-weeks old baby, then 3 buses to classes at York University, then repeat that in the evenings – 12 bus rides per day!), she was the one who offered to come to my house to babysit our daughter to make it easier for me. Needless to say, she and her husband are our daughter's God-parents, (along with another sister-friend Cynthia C. who lives in New York). In all of those ventures

Charm did not ask and was not given a penny. She knew we had very little! God was our provider!

And the LORD said unto Moses, Wherefore criest thou unto me? speak unto the children of Israel, that they go forward. But lift thou up thy rod, and stretch out thine hand over the sea, and divide it: and the children of Israel shall go on dry ground through the midst of the sea (Ex. 14: 15-16).

It is time to go forward under God's providential care! Lift up your rod. Stretch forth your hand. The pains, hurts, anxieties, worries in your life will go. The heavy waters will subside. It is time to go through on dry land.

God's care is sure. God's name MUST be glorified. He will not go back on His word. *God is not a man, that he should lie; neither the son of man, that he should repent: hath he said, and shall he not do it? or hath he spoken, and shall he not make it good* (Num. 23:19)? The believer will always experience triumph. A few lines of one of my favorite songs says, "Victory, Victory shall be mine – if I just hold my peace and let the Lord fight my battles, victory shall be mine".

As we go forward, let us call ourselves to less murmuring and more trusting in His providential care. "*Trust in the Lord with all thy might, Lean not to your own understanding and he shall direct your path* (Prov. 3: 5-6). God has fought many battles. He has never lost one. God will fight for you and no matter how it seems, with God, you will never lose.

Your enemies will be defeated. Your improbable circumstances will be made whole. "*Israel saw that great work which the Lord did upon the Egyptians: and the people feared the Lord, and believed the Lord, and his servant Moses* (Prov. 14:.31).

My anxiety about who would take care of our child was resolved. God sent a good person who cared, into our lives. The Israelites' worries about how they would cross the red sea was taken care of. God always goes ahead of us to prepare the way. His providential care is always at work. I was able to go to school without worry; I knew our daughter was in good hands. The Israelites walked on dry land and then saw the Egyptians dead as they were covered by water. They saw the mighty hand of God and they feared the Lord and believed the Lord. His name must be glorified in all life's circumstances. Allow Him to have His Providential will in your life.

When you receive a true revelation of God's majesty and His sovereignty, you will follow Him in faith while growing and abiding in His presence. Go forward in the strength and security of our mighty God!

Prison Walls Are Shaking

"Cribb'd, cabin'd and chain'd"
Like worthy Macbeth of old
Meshed in a prison – a mirage of thoughts
Finances are short
Miracles don't happen anymore

No more praying,
No more fasting,
Painfully engulfed – body and soul
Entrenched with anger and despair
Lord, where do I go? To whom do I turn?

Those prison walls are shaking!
Rumbling loud and clear!
That angel has come!
Give your hand – be lead!

Out of your prison
Shake off those chains
You're free – bird-like: loose!
The shackles are broken
Those prison walls are down!
Miracles still happen!

A LIFE WORTH LIVING - DESPITE THE ODDS

Scripture Meditation
Ecclesiastes 1

Early in our lives my husband and I learnt that trusting God was always important, no matter how desperate our situation seemed. The first terrible experience we had in the brutal Toronto winter was not a pleasant one. My husband was what you would call "pounding the pavement" looking for jobs. We lived at Wasdale Crescent. He left home early every morning, went to literally every business place he could find to seek employment. It was cold – freezing on this day. His coat was thin (couldn't afford a thick one), gloves also were thin. After a day in the cold, he ended up in the Landsdowne and St. Clair Avenue area, (about a 2.5 hour walk to our home, 2 busses). Of course he had to walk because he had no money to pay his fare! Heavenly father! Walking ten minutes in that weather would have been terrible, not to mention two and a half hours! He walked into the apartment and his body parts were frozen! His hands and feet were burning – hard and frozen. I, the good wife, the new immigrant who had no idea what to do in this situation, did the only thing I could think of. I got a kettle full of hot water and proceeded to "warm" him down with a towel soaked in hot water. I heard the most excruciating cry I had ever heard in my life! The hot water was no good for his frozen body. We both cried and cried as his frozen body thawed.

One of the major themes in the book of Ecclesiastes is about human sufferings and their frailties.

The opening verse begins with a picture of despair; Chapter 1:2 *"Vanity of vanity, saith the Preacher, vanity of vanities, all is vanity." The Hebrew word being referenced here is "vapor"*

For the most part, the Book of Psalms is filled with optimism. Then you get to Proverbs, which is also filled with optimism as it illustrates the importance of true wisdom guided by God. Then suddenly, here we are in Ecclesiastes which is filled with pessimism. The Preacher questions the justice of God, when the righteous suffers, even sometimes at the hand of the wicked.

Life's experiences – A frozen body from walking in the snow, death, suffering, discouragement, loss of friends or family, loss of possession, loss of hope, and even loneliness, can sometimes cripple our minds. These are images that convey hopelessness and futility. The Preacher expresses that generations come and generations go, but the earth remains forever. In other words, life is cyclical. It repeats itself. Nothing really changes. No progress is made. Babies are born; the elderly die; there is nothing new *under the sun.*

He continues his discourse, that basically, longings of the human heart are never fulfilled. They are never really satisfied. The eye never sees enough; the ear never hears enough. Life is like chasing the wind. The futility of that imagery (vapor-like) is evident. We are unable to catch it; it's always evading.

Having looked then at all this doom and gloom, we are left to ponder: *What is the reason for us to be alive? What is the purpose of trying to acquire anything? What is it that keeps people from committing mass suicide? What is it that keeps us from deciding to curse God and die like Job's wife counseled? What is the purpose of even serving God?*

There is only one resounding answer in all this. Deeper than the despair that anyone can experience, there must be an underlying reverence for God and faith in His word, and faith in His ability to control the universe.

How does one continue to have faith in God amidst all this despair? A view of God makes everything around us look different. In Genesis Chapter 22, we are reminded that He is our Jehovah Jireh – our provider. In Genesis 17:1 & 2, He is our El Shaddai – God Almighty; and in Exodus 12:22-26 He is our Jehovah Rophe – One that heals. All this conveys the message that He is totally capable and can take care of every aspect of our lives. When one gets a glimpse of God, therefore, we understand that He is able to turn our darkness to light, our sorrows to joy, mourning and weeping to laughter, disappointments to hope, and degenerated lives to regenerated lives.

There is no need to settle for despair, even amidst the doom and gloom of the beginning of Ecclesiastes. We are told that, *He hath made everything beautiful in his time: also he hath set the word in their heart, so that no man can find out the work that God maketh from the beginning to the end* (Eccl. 3:1). The Preacher acknowledges that God is eternal. If God is eternal, then all things are in His control! This includes fears, doubts, disappointments, and sorrows. He has us all in his hands and will see His children through, despite all odds.

Amidst life's follies and disappointments: loss of job, lack of money, broken homes, broken marriages, unruly children, abandoned friendships, we are called upon to, *fear God and keep His commandments for this is the whole duty of man* (Eccl. 12:13).

The depressing observations of the early chapters of Ecclesiastes are made with the natural eyes. How often, today we make similar observations when God is working on our behalf and in our finiteness we are not sure what He is doing. When we view with our natural eyes, situations seem hopeless! Burdens seem heavier! Foes seem greater! But God promises to take care of us; *He is not slack concerning his promise as some men count slackness* (2 Pet. 3:9).

When we become conscious of the awesomeness of God and consider His omnipotence, we can bask in the assurance that He is able. He undergirds us; and when thoughts of disillusionment try to invade our minds, his manifold care shines through.

Why art thou cast down, O my soul? And why art thou disquieted within me? Hope thou in God: for I will praise him, who is the healer of my countenance and my God (Ps. 42:11). The soul that is in despair must begin to praise God. He can be anyone you want Him to be in your life.

Life is meaningless without Him. The doom and despair of the first chapters of Ecclesiastes is what life is like without Christ. The vanity and vapour-like quality of life can be changed to a meaningful life. To Christians who are experiencing defeat in your lives, God can change that. He can restore the joy that the enemy of your soul has robbed. Stand! Pray! Trust! And see God work for you!

Battered, Broken, Not Defeated

I stand aghast
Battered and broken
Withered and melted from the heat of life
Cold and shivering from the freeze
I wonder what next
Sun won't shine, rain comes pelting
I stand hollow and frail

All this only for a season I'm told
Nothing lasts for Ever
Only Salvation, they say
Then I will wait and pray
Chains brake through prayer
That is for sure!

I stand muted
Waiting, Waiting, Waiting, Hoping
Will she ever come . . . Hope?
Change? Better? What next?
Now a glimpse of light
It gets bigger . . . and bigger . . .

I stand above it all
Transformed, renewed, strengthened
Hope and Change have come!
What light to chart my path!
This path seems clear
I will embrace!

POSSESS THE LAND

Scripture Meditation
Numbers 13

God spoke to Moses to send twelve men, one from each of the tribes of Israel to search the land of Canaan. The men brought back a branch of grape to signify the fruitfulness of the land. They also brought back good tidings; *surely it* (the land) *floweth with milk and honey,* and showing the grape, proclaimed, *this is the fruit of it* (Num.13:27).

It is noteworthy to consider that even when we see with our very eyes what God has done for us and the blessings He bestows upon us daily, we are still tempted to doubt Him. We tend to limit His Supremacy to the dictates of our frail finite minds. Thus, the people began to look at what they perceived as insurmountable barriers. *Nevertheless the people be strong that dwell in the land, and the cities are walled, and very great: and moreover we saw the children of Anak there* (Num13:28). Surprisingly, many of us live daily in a state of "Nevertheless". No matter what God says to us through His word and songs, we still say "nevertheless". "Alas! He might still not be able to do as He says!" We wake up every day audibly hailing God for what he is able to do, looking at the "grapes" and boasting of the promise of "milk and honey", yet continue to live in "Nevertheless" land with our actions.

Despite the fruitfulness of the land, all we can focus on at times is *"the strong"* people that dwell in the land, the *"walled cities"* and the *"children of Anak"*. Notably, there were "giants" in the land; but what these people forgot, and what we tend to forget at times, is that our God is stronger than any man, can scale any high wall and is not afraid of giants. He is the conquering Lion of the tribe of Judah!

When faced with our high walls and giants, instead of taking matters in our own hands and diverting from the path, when God has already given us orders to go, let us go as He has commanded. When He sends us into a "land", He already knows the size of the giants who live there. He already knows the high walls we have to overcome, but if He sends us, He has already prepared the way. No matter how strong your opposition is, God's might is stronger. *He giveth power to the faint; and to them that have no might he increaseth strength* (Isa. 40:29).

All oppositional high walls must crumble when God is in control. Too many times we are fearful of the "walls" which prevent us from possessing the "land" that God has promised us. "Land" in our lives could be jobs, relationships, marriages, finances and any other thing that we desire from God. He is telling us to go in His name and possess that land! Do not focus on the walls of discouragements and disappointments. Do not worry about the strong people who are naysayers and are waiting for you to fail. All of these must crumble in the presence of God. He has already told you the "land" will be yours, and He has already made the way for you to possess it.

It is time to march around those walls seven times. They must come down with your shout! God says, "**Go forward and possess the land**"; regardless of the "*walled cities*".

Despite some negative reports, Caleb, "*stilled the people before Moses, and said, Let us go up at once, and possess it; for we are well able to overcome it* (Num. 13: 30).

It is time for us to follow God's direction and go up and possess the land. We are well able. Let us dispel our fears of the "giants' the "walled cities" and the "strong men" in our lives. Our God is well able and with Him, we are too!

VICTIMS OR VICTORS # I

Our Faith- The Anchor Holds

Scripture Meditation
Zechariah 4:6
Then he answered and spake unto me, saying,
This is the word of the Lord unto Zerubbabel,
saying, Not by might, nor by power, but
by my spirit, saith the Lord of hosts.
Matthew 28:18
And Jesus came and spake unto them, saying, All
power is given unto me in heaven and in earth.

My husband would go out at 5:00 every morning to the Employment
Agency in Montreal. Someone had to earn. I was in full-time school.
Each morning I would pray, "Lord please let him find a job today". It
was day by day. Every day he didn't work would be one for which we
would not have that money at the end of the month. The rent for our
little one-bedroom apartment was not much, but when you do not
have anything, everything is much! I would lie in bed hopeful, praying
not to hear that door open after 8:00 a.m., as if it did, that would
mean he didn't get a job for that day. Imagine the disappointment I
experienced when I would hear the door open at 9:00. The poor thing!
He would come home with his head bowed, and we both would look
at each other, wouldn't say a word; but our dismayed expression said
it all. But at the end of each month, our rent was always paid and we
always had food. A little old lady, (Sis. B.) in our church saw us, two
"trying" young people in our twenties. The Lord touched her heart

and she would come to us, would hold each of our hands and say, "You rent pay?" We would answer "yes" in unison; then she would say, "Alright, take this and buy some grocery", leaving folded dollar bills in our hands. Thank God for people with the gift of giving! Many years after, we found ourselves playing the role of Sis. B. Had we succumbed to the disappointments of those day, we would not be here rejoicing today. By trusting God we were victorious over many situations, even those that seemed hopeless.

Victims or Victors - these are two very powerful words in the English Language with which we struggle, in essence, on a daily basis. We might not actually say the words but we act them out daily in various situations. As we struggle through life with all its highs and lows we are constantly reminded that there is a constant warring, a constant fight, internally, and yes, sometimes externally.

By definition: Victim - *somebody who or something that is adversely affected by an action or circumstance;* and Victor - *a winner in a contest or battle.* Consider for a moment the various things that have kept you from living a victorious life, whether as a child, husband, father, mother, wife, Christian, or in the other various roles you play.

For some situations in which we find ourselves, we immediately feel like victims; because instead of giving them to God we take them on to ourselves. Zechariah 4:6, however, reminds us that we will not win victories because of our own valour or ability, *not by might or by power, but by my power, saith the Lord.* Rom. 6:16 serves as the key to many answers that plague us about living a victorious life. *Know ye not, that to whom ye yield yourselves servants to obey, his servants ye are to whom ye obey; whether of sin unto death, or of obedience unto righteousness?* Here Paul warns believers who think they can be victorious yet continue to live a sinful life because they are under grace. If we give ourselves to sin we will become slaves to sin and continue to live as victims; the result of which is everlasting death!

Many times, in considering whether we are victims or victors we ask ourselves questions like, Why does the devil seem so powerful in my life? As my son Scott points out to me, we give the devil too much credit. The bigger question, however, is: Whose servants are we, God's or Devil's? In order to be victorious what will we choose - Sin or Righteousness? We should take time to examine our thoughts, motives, morals, and actions, and earnestly strive to ensure that they are controlled by truth and righteousness and not by depravity and unrighteousness.

God will not force us to live right and be victorious. Satan will not force us to be victims. The devil has no power; he only seems powerful because so many people yield to him in their victim-filled lives.

The choice is ours! God is the only source of true power, and as such, the only source of our victory. *All power is given unto me in heaven and in earth* (Matt. 28:18). God's people are promised authority over darkness, and given the power to proclaim the word of God throughout the world. We need to live within the means of that power in order to be victorious

The path we choose will determine if we live our lives as victims or victors? If we choose to submit to truth and righteousness we are choosing the path to a victor's life. Conversely, if we chose to live in sin and unrighteousness we are choosing the path to a defeated victim-like life.

There is no middle ground! We are either on God's side – victor, or on the devil's side – victim!
And *if it seem evil unto you to serve the LORD, choose you this day whom ye will serve; whether the gods which your fathers served that were on the other side of the flood, or the gods of the Amorites, in whose land ye dwell: but as for me and my house, we will serve the LORD* (Josh. 24:15).

The Open Window

Standing at the window, my eyes piercing the
Horizon
What is beyond, I wonder
God only knows – He the all-knowing, the Almighty
Blue skies enchanting
Where do they start? Where do they end?
Birds rustling to and fro – freedom they beckon
I stand at the window – an open window
Do I go or do I stay?

Winged thoughts now return
"My life is in your hand", I say aloud
The future, though unknown, becomes clear
Insurmountable odds, I'm now able to conquer
Windows of my thoughts now flown widely open
I must go through, through the open window – Wow!
It suddenly becomes a door!
He is the Door!

VICTIMS OR VICTORS # II

Playing Our Part as the Holy Spirit Works

Scripture Meditation
Romans 7

In order to live a victorious Christian life we must do a number of things, one of which is, we must yield to the Holy Spirit. Because there is a constant warring of flesh and spirit, we must continuously ask God to allow the Holy Spirit to dominate our lives, our thoughts, our actions and our motives. Paul states, *I find then a law, that, when I would do good, evil is present with me* (Rom. 7:21). In verse 24, Paul cries out, *O wretched man that I am.* The unregenerated person, after maintaining a losing conflict against sin, after falling victim to the devil and his wiles, cries out in anguish – *O wretched man that I am.*

The only person who can rescue us from this life of defeat is Jesus Christ, through the Holy Spirit. The life that is yielded to God has power over the world, sin, and the devil. Christians do not have to continue to live a life of futility and hopelessness - defeated and depraved. *Greater is He that is within us than He that is in the world* (1 John 4:4b). With this understanding, we can conquer the mountains we face.

In order to be victorious we must allow the Holy Spirit to tear down strongholds so that God can release us into victory. *Submit yourselves therefore to God. Resist the devil, and he will flee from you* (Jas. 4:7). It is time to pull down strongholds in our lives, no matter what those are. Each individual knows his or her stronghold. It is time to resist the devil in whatever form he appears.

One of the most imminent strongholds in our lives that prevent us from living a victorious Christian life is double-mindedness: part God and part world; a "little sin", and "a little righteousness". That is a colossal remedy for defeat! God is a jealous God and when we serve Him we must do so whole-heartedly in truth and righteousness. We must *draw near with a true heart in full assurance of faith, having our hearts sprinkled from an evil conscience, and our bodies washed with pure water* (Heb. 10:22). We are admonished, not to *bow down thyself to them (other gods), nor serve them: for I the LORD thy God am a jealous God, visiting the iniquity of the fathers upon the children unto the third and fourth generation of them that hate me* (Deut. 5:9).

Consider also other strongholds that prevent us from being victors. According to Titus 3:3, they include being foolish, deceived, disobedient, immoral, and prideful. Along with those, being hateful of others, adhering to divers lusts and pleasures, and living in malice and envy are traits that will allow us to live a victim-filled life.

To be victors, we must allow the Holy Spirit to do the job that He is placed in our lives to do. *And when he is come, he will reprove the world of sin, and of righteousness, and of judgment* (John 16:8). Reprove means to expose, refute or convince. We must allow the Holy Spirit to convict our hearts and bring us salvation, and into true servant-hood. *No man can say that Jesus is Lord, but by the Holy Spirit* (1 Cor. 12:3). Clearly, by the same token, no man can live victoriously but by, and through the person of the Holy Spirit.

VICTIMS OR VICTORS # III

Living a victorious Christian Life

Scripture Meditation
Ephesians 2:2; 1Peter 1:2b-7

Coming from what I consider a middle class home where as long as I can remember we always had someone working with us, someone Jamaicans call the "Helper", I entered a new reality when I came to Canada. As you will notice throughout my anecdotes, lack of money was a key factor in our early years in Canada (something I did not experience in Jamaica,). As a second year student at York I decided to do odd jobs, including housekeeping on the days I had no classes. I entered a woman's house; I noticed the diploma on the wall for her son who had graduated from York University. My thoughts in Jamaican patois, "She no know sa mi a Yark student to" – (translation: "Doesn't she know that I am also a York University student"). Of course not, I am her housekeeper! Needless to say, by the end of the second day she paid me and told me she didn't think I was "cut out for this job". I was fired!

My mother came to visit for the summer as she did every year. I tried to hide the fact from her that I was cleaning offices in the evenings, as I needed to earn some money. Somehow she found out. My friend Marian S., my batch mate from Teachers' College was also visiting. One evening we decided that all three of us would go do my office cleaning job. In the middle of our work my mom stopped and observed, "Patsie (as I am called at times), these offices are very important, they have a nurse and two teachers cleaning them!" We all had a good laugh! One just had to do what one needed to do!

Returning to school in the Fall, I signed up with an agency to work on my days off from class (needless to say I should not be doing that, as I only had a student visa, and no work permit)! Oh I got a babysitting job alright. Two days per week! On the 3rd day I had the baby on the change table, trying to balance her as I searched the draw for pampers! What do you know! The child slid right under my hand and landed on the floor! Mom came running in (note: I was already warned by the agency that she is mildly schizophrenic), screaming, "Did you drop her, did you drop her", getting louder by the second! I stood there speechless, so she knew. In her loudest voice she started screaming and pointing to the door, "GET OUT! GET OUT"! I still remember, feeling totally defeated walking to Danforth Subway, crying and wondering . . . does God care.

Victorious living can only be achieved when as Christians we commit our ways to Christ. We must form an intimate relationship with Him as we experience the New Birth and start a new relationship. True confession of unconfessed sins is a good place to begin. Once that is done, it behooves us to no longer entertain the spirit of Satan and defeat which works in children of disobedience.

In time past ye walked according to the course of this world, according to the prince of the power of the air, the spirit that now worketh in the children of disobedience (Eph. 2:2) That was our past. Without Christ it is impossible to be victorious, as we are all "controlled by the Prince of the power of the air" i.e. Satan. Without Christ's protection, one is "enslaved" to sin and the craving of one's sinful nature, thus, one becomes victim to Satan. With Christ we are different. We are made whole. We are victors!

The secret of victorious Christian living is found in the excellence of our relationship with Christ through the Holy Spirit. It is not found in the type of job we do, cleaning offices or homes, baby-sitting a screaming child, being a teacher, nurse, doctor or any other job. Our status has no significance in the scheme of being a victor in Christ. Those and similar things are stepping stones to our victory, but it behooves us not to get bogged down with those harsh realities which will prevent us from living a victorious life in Christ. As long as Christ is within a person, he or she does not only live triumphantly now, but has future glory of eternal life. God has made abundant provision for everyone to live victoriously. 1 Peter 1 reminds us of our "incorruptible inheritance" which does not fade away and is reserved for us in heaven. We can therefore rejoice that this awaits us if we continue to live a victorious Christian life.

Victim or Victor? *Therefore seeing we have this ministry, as we have received mercy, we faint not* (2 Cor. 4:1). We are also reminded that though our "outward man" perishes, the "inward man" is renewed daily. It is time to refrain from half-hearted Christianity which allows us to live in defeat as victims. The choice is ours. It is time to be "completely sold out" to Christ and bask in His victories. God's will for every person is that each of us live in victory through the power and person of the Holy Spirit.

What is your resolve today? Will you be a Victim or Victor?

Light Overcomes Dark

Thoughts ravishing my brain
Menacing darkness creeps in with the night
Dark, Dark, Dark . . .

Where is Hope?
Where has peace gone? They've left me behind - alone
I turn for Joy and she is absent too
Who's left? What is left?
Hopelessness and despair
Walking through a dark valley
The night is long . . . it goes on and on . . .
Night can't last forever
The day must dawn, I know it!

Still awake from the long night
I can see little bolts of light fighting through the dark
Fight on good friend
Then slowly light starts creeping through the night approaching dawn
Hope returns from his long journey
His friend Joy and Peace follow suit
Light comes

I can now search for green pastures
They await me
Someone I can trust is holding my hand . . . Leading me
I am ready to go! Go I must!

Oh the light shines brighter and brighter
It is the dawn of a new day
Light shines bright
In my heart!
In my mind!
In my spirit!
In my thoughts!

The Master of the universe says, Yes!
You are my child. I am your light.
I am your peace!
I am your joy!

THE LORD IS MY SHEPHERD # 1

He Protects Us and Takes Care of Our Needs

Scripture Meditation
Psalms 23

It was the day I pledged in my heart that I was going to buy the Lottery. You have to understand that all my life I was taught that gambling is a sin, and was also taught that buying the lottery was a sin! I didn't care! I needed money and I was going to buy it! I stood at the counter in the Yonge and Sheppard Mall and as I waited in line, tears literally flowed down my cheeks. I had come to the end of the road waiting on God, and my school fee (International student school fee – almost 2 times the norm for regular Canadian students) had to be paid! I had got some money from my friend who I will call Sonia F. who lived in Montreal at the time, but it was just not enough! As I waited in the Lotto ticket line, tears running down, I literally felt like someone came, held my hand and walked me out of the line. I left without buying a ticket and went home.

At the time, I lived at Keele and Wilson Avenue. There was a CIBC bank at the corner where we did our banking. A few days later I went to the bank (to do our little banking) and when my passbook was updated I noticed that there was much more money in it than I could account for. I called this to the Teller's attention. She asked if I had any one depositing money into my account, I answered "no". She advised me to let it be, "it would correct itself eventually, someone will find the mistake," she said. Days passed. I kept returning to the bank to enquire. They refused to pull the money from my account as they wouldn't know where to put it (the law of debit and credit). I asked to speak to the Manager, she could do nothing. Months passed and I watched my passbook literally every day to see when they would correct the mistake and pull the money from my account. Remember now, my school fee had still not been paid. I was just drooling for the money and there was more than enough now in my account to pay it. No one in the bank would touch that money. I started sharing with people and I got various types of advice, e.g. "Take out the money and close the account". (No, I can't do that, it's not my money). After many months and repeated efforts (which I carefully documented) to draw the attention of the bank personnel to situation, I decided to tread the water. I bought a money order from my account for York University. Needless to say I waited with baited breath for months, going into years to have someone correct that "erroneous" deposit in my account. No one ever said a word! It has been almost 41 years! People have told me (may be in jest – but something to consider) "God saw that you needed the money and deposited it for you!" To this day that is still a mystery to me, but He did say He is my Shepherd and I shall lack nothing!

Psalms 23 speaks of the confidence we have in God's grace and care. It was written and sung by David, not when he fled into the forest of Hareth (1 Sam. l 22:5), as some Hebrews will have it; but when, having overcome all his enemies, and settled his kingdom, he enjoyed great peace and quiet. It expresses personal confidence, joy, and triumph, from beginning to end. God's people then, and today have their seasons of darkness and their times of rejoicing.

One image Jesus used often in His ministry was that of a shepherd. This was a common image to which people in his day could easily relate. The shepherd goes before, not merely to point out the way, but to see that it is feasible and safe. He is armed in order to defend his charge, and in this he is very courageous. Many adventures with wild beasts occur, similar to what is recounted by David (1 Sam. 27:34-36).

In the narrative in Psalm 23, David extols the goodness of God as his shepherd. He expresses his confidence in Him. As our Shepherd He feeds, guides, governs, and defends us, his flock. Interestingly, this follows Psalms 22nd, which is peculiarly the Psalms of the Cross. There are no green pastures, no still waters in Ps.22.

After reading, "My God, my God, why hast thou forsaken me?" (Ps. 22) we come to "The Lord is my Shepherd."

God allows Himself to be compared to anything which will set forth his great love and care for his people. David had himself been a keeper of sheep, and understood both the needs of the sheep and the many upkeeps of a shepherd. David compares himself to a creature, fragile, powerless, and foolish; and he takes God to be his Provider, Preserver, Director, and indeed, his everything.

A Good Shepherd knows the sheep by name and calls them by it, *My sheep listen to my voice; I know them, and they follow me* (John 10:27).

A pastor is a shepherd to the church. An elder or deacon is a shepherd in the body. A husband is a shepherd to his wife. Parents are shepherds to their children. A teacher is a shepherd to his or her students. An employer is a shepherd to the employees. An older child is a shepherd to his younger siblings. YET in all of these shepherding relationships, Christ the Good Shepherd supersedes all. He gave his life for His sheep.

With joy the Psalmist reflects that he has a shepherd, and that shepherd is Jehovah who is able to take care of his every need. There is no "if" nor "but" when David says, *The Lord is my shepherd.* He immediately follows that with a most reassuring statement, he shall "lack nothing".

We must cultivate the spirit of assured dependence upon our heavenly Father. *"My"* implies personal relationship! He cares for *me,* watches over *me,* and preserves *me.* He is *my* feeder, *my* nourisher, and my sustainer. He supplies *my* every need out of His heart full of love. He will not withhold anything from me. Temporal or spiritual, we shall have no lack. *The young lions do lack, and suffer hunger: but they that seek the Lord shall not want any good thing* (Ps. 34:10). His grace is truly sufficient for me.

We need to rise above our fears and wants by committing ourselves to the care of the Good Shepherd, not by placing our confidence in worldly things. As in my anecdote, we must understand that God knows our needs and He will take care of them. Our Shepherd is all-sufficient. Through famine or calamity *"I shall not want"*. Even death with its gloom shall not find us in despair.

He reminds us as His sheep that, *when thou passest through the waters, I will be with thee; and through the rivers, they shall not overflow thee* (Isa. 43:2). He takes us in "green pasture", allowing us repose for peace and rest. There is both delight and plenty of provisions rich in vegetation; not parched, barren land. To the unregenerated man, the greatest abundance is but parched pastures, but to a godly man, who is led in green pasture, there is daily peace and contentment. His emphasis is not on transient things, but rather on his eternal reward.

In "still waters" there is the suggestion of peace. His Spirit cleanses and refreshes. When in still waters, our neighbors may not understand our peace and calm in the midst of chaos, as God continually restores our soul and leads us in paths of righteousness. He wants us to be holy. He brings us back from our erroneous wanderings. He brings peace to our weary heart *and* replaces despair with hope; even when the world is in turmoil. When our soul grows sorrowful, He revives it; when it is sinful, He sanctifies it; and when it is weak He strengthens it.

When our Good Shepherd is leading us, we are not afraid of valleys or mountains, no matter how treacherous. We need not be afraid of the fiery darts of Satan that he shoots from the mountain when we are in the valley. His "rod" and his "staff" are designed to protect and guide us. We are not fearful of even death. We go through the gloomy tunnel of death and emerge into the light of immortality. Even then we do not fear as we have our Good Shepherd as our guide.

THE LORD IS MY SHEPHERD # II

He Blesses in Abundance

Scripture Meditation
Psalms 23

Daily we are encouraged that our Shepherd furnishes us with provisions, and comforts us so that our cup "runneth over". This overflowing suggests the fullness and abundance we have in God. In spite of, and in the sight of our enemies, God prepares us a table with sumptuous meals. How refreshing is this assurance! What provision He makes for His sheep! To date, I still have no idea where that deposit came from, but after all these years, I firmly believe God saw our needs and made provision for us. Let us continue to live in the daily fresh anointing. Our friends, neighbours and acquaintances must know when we are being led by this Good Shepherd. They must see the anointing on our lives. They should see our cups running over; cups of joy, cups of praise, cups of thanksgiving, cups of peace and loving kindness. These should exemplify our walk with the Good Shepherd. What a joy to bask in the knowledge and comfort that "goodness" and "mercy" shall always be ours!

We should keep near our shepherd, and follow His leading without hesitation. We should not stray or loiter far behind; and if we do, we should heed to Him as He turns around and scolds us. The shepherd calls sharply from time to time to remind us of his presence. We should know His voice, and follow on; but, if a stranger calls, we should not heed. In following the Good Shepherd, we experience

His limitless protection and provision, and are assured daily of His goodness towards us. We also experience deliverance from death; so though this vessel of clay shall cease, we have hope of another body. Let us continue to stay under the umbrella of the Good Shepherd, no matter how rough the field gets and no matter how tempted we are to stray.

Light Wins Again

The sun sets in the West
Shadows crawl, then hasten
Night creeps stealthily along. . . ruining the day
Soon darkness engulfs

Sleep transpires, tranquility for some
Reckless dreams and unconscious wanderings for others
Somber restlessness

But soon the darkness passes
And the sun and light creep through the cracks
In windows, through curtains, doors and to the heart
Light and hope ensue
The sun shines once again
Hearts are merry – a BRIGHTER day has dawned
Hope and Light overpower gloom and dark

Hope wins again
Peace wins again
Joy wins too
Light wins again!

THE CHRISTIAN'S JOURNEY # I

Packing Excess Baggage

Scripture Meditation
Hebrews 12: 21

Wherefore seeing we also are compassed about with so great a cloud of witnesses, let us lay aside every weight, and the sin which doth so easily beset us, and let us run with patience the race that is set before us.

As we prepare for literal trips, whether they are for 1 week or more, we pack suitcases with all kinds of items, checking and double checking that we do not forget important items. Realistically though, if you are like me, you always over pack, getting to your destination and realizing that you didn't need half the clothes and shoes you brought! I would pack fifteen casual shirts and a few "in-betweens" for my husband, at least fifteen tops and matching shorts, plus dresses for myself - for a 7-day trip! My sons when they are going on a one week vacation would pack a different pair of sneakers for each day! They would have ten pairs of jeans for a seven-day trip! Excessive! My daughter, on the other hand, would pack just enough for the week, and occasionally, half way through the week she would be knocking on my door to borrow a top. Where is the middle ground? Should we pack too much, too little, or just enough?

So it is with our Christian Journey. Christians pack so much at times that they become burdened down with the load, and the journey gets wearisome. In many instances the spiritual suitcases are full of malice, envy, slandering, lying, covetousness, secularism, murmuring, complaining and you name it! Where as in the literal trip we probably just have to pay a minimal fine for overweight; packing too much on the Christian journey can be very detrimental to building our relationship with God. As Christians, our luggage should have no place for unhealthy characteristics and practices. We should guard our hearts and minds so that malice, envy and such the likes are not part of what we carry on our Christian journey.

It is time to do inventory; to STOP and start unpacking. *Now ye also put off all these; anger, wrath, malice, blasphemy, filthy communication out of your mouth. Lie not one to another, seeing that ye have put off the old man with his* deeds (Col. 3:8-9). We are also admonished that, *seeing we also are compassed about with so great a cloud of witnesses, let us lay aside every weight, and the sin which doth so easily beset us, and let us run with patience the race that is set before us* (Heb. 12:1). How can we run well when our suit cases and back packs are heavily weighing us down?

On this pathway, one of the most important things is that we must get rid of some of the excess baggage that our human frame allows us to carry along. As we strive to get rid of the unnecessary weight, we must be mindful that we refill the spaces with things that we will definitely need for a successful journey and which we cannot have in excess. Let us, *put on therefore, as the elect of God, holy and beloved, bowels of mercies, kindness, humbleness of mind, meekness, longsuffering . . . Let the word of Christ dwell in you richly in all wisdom; teaching and admonishing one another in psalms and hymns and spiritual songs, singing with grace in your hearts to the Lord* (Col. 3:12-16).

The Highway of Holiness is for whomever will travel on it, but will not accommodate the baggage of sin as the cited verse indicates; *the unclean shall not travel on it.* This includes not only unclean sinners, who have not accepted Christ as personal Saviour; but it also includes the carnal Christians who continue to walk in unconfessed and uncleansed sin. What will you carry on this journey?

THE CHRISTIAN'S JOURNEY # II

Signs on the Highway

Scripture Meditation

Proverbs 14:12
There is a way which seemeth right unto a man,
but the end thereof are the ways of death.

Isiah 35:8
And an highway shall be there, and a way, and it
shall be called The way of holiness; the unclean
shall not pass over it; but it shall be for those: the
wayfaring men, though fools, shall not err therein.

In our earlier years in Canada when we just started a family, we did many road trips from Canada to the U.S. to visit family members (mainly because we couldn't afford airfare for all of us). It was much cheaper to drive, and frankly, we had lots of fun; our children still look back on those with fond memories. We would leave very early in the mornings, around 4:00 a.m. so that we would get a good way on our journey before the sun rose and the heavy traffic began. The first part of our journey was relatively quiet because the children would still be sleeping, tucked in with their comforters and pillows.

As soon as we did a breakfast stop, maybe four hours into the journey, everyone would be wide awake. Scott, our youngest was pretty quiet, he was still pretty much a baby (by the time he got older we were able to afford more air travel). The two older children, Trevlin and Richard, however, became our navigators. That is of course between fights for personal space and their dad threatening to tie one of them on the top of the car, if the fighting continued. They would focus on the road for a while and that was when Richard who wanted to show off his reading skills, much to Trevlin's annoyance, would read every road sign aloud. At points we would get to an exit sign and even though it was not our exit, he would shout out "mom, dad, the sign says exit." Then we would explain, that was not our exit. The exciting part was when they got hungry and needed a service station, then the mile countdown would begin. Every mile past we would hear, ten, nine, eight ... down to zero, and then there would be a big cheer from the back of the car when we pulled into the service station. We would get back on the highway, and their reading of the road signs began again, until silence came from the back of the car because everyone would be fast asleep, even with Trevlin's best effort to stay awake.

Life's highways are also filled with signs to which we must adhere. These highways can be fraught with dangers at different times. When the warning signs appear, we should obey them. If the sign says that the bridge is dangerous to cross over, we should take the alternate route. Turn aside. If the weatherman says to stay indoors and not drive, then we should try not to drive that day. If the sign says, "slippery road", we aim to drive slowly and carefully. We heed the signs.

God has given us a road map with signs for travelling on the Spiritual Highway. It is His desire that everyone who confesses his or her sin and accepts Him as Saviour, reaches the same destination, which is our heavenly home. Everyone is on a different road with different markers. It has always amazed me as I travelled from Canada to the U.S by car to see some people go at extremely high speed, while others drive slower, cautiously obeying the speed limits. So it is with the travelers on the Spiritual Highway. Some people are cruising at 80-100 km; while others are going faster or slower, obeying or disobeying the speed limit (all the things that God wants us to do to present ourselves holy before Him). Where ever you are on this journey, be certain that your unseen driver is the Holy Spirit Himself, leading you to the same destination – eternal life with your creator!

When travelling on the highway and we see the sign "wrong way", we immediately stop to think. We instinctively do not keep going, as we know if we continue, there might be danger ahead. Similarly, many times on our Christian journey, God, through various means, (a song, a prayer, a message), calls out "wrong way" to us, yet we keep going in the same direction which could ultimately lead to head-on crashes!

Let us take this moment to STOP and heed the road signs on this Christian path. The road you are on now might look smooth. Everything is fine, a nice job, a beautiful car, loving family, great friends, lots of money, and just about everything you think you need to be happy; but God is still saying WRONG WAY! The truth is, if God is not on this road with you, you are heading the wrong way. Without God, everything is meaningless. You are still steering the car heading for a precipice.

It is time for a U-TURN! On the Christian journey we cannot afford to trust our own instinct. God has already given us a road map – the Bible. The cited scripture reminds us that though that way seems right to us, it could lead to death. We need to YEILD to what God is saying to us. Sometimes this YEILDING involves making a DETOUR or taking a U-TURN; but it must happen, in order to correct our path.

The question that confronts everyone is: "How long will you continue to travel on the road you are on, even though the DANGER AHEAD sign is flashing; and the RED LIGHT is solid? If we continue to run through those red lights in our lives we are heading right into a CRASH!! When God says STOP, He means STOP! In order to have a successful journey, God must lead the way. *Trust in the LORD with all thine heart; and lean not unto thine own understanding. In all thy ways acknowledge him, and he shall direct thy paths* (Prov. 3:5-6)

Sometimes on this journey there might be needs or desires for DETOURS. God knows all our detours, even before we come upon them. There are times when we go out of His will and stray from the path He has planned for us. Be assured, however, that there is a PATH that leads you back to the main path. In Job 23:10, Job says, *but he knoweth the way that I take: when he hath tried me, I shall come forth as gold.*

As we travel on this Spiritual Highway, there are some road signs that we MUST adhere to for a safe journey. We must understand on this highway there is only ONE WAY to the ultimate destination. John 14:3 states, *And if I go and prepare a place for you, I will come again, and receive you unto myself; that where I am, there ye may be also.* Sometimes going on a trip, especially if you are not the driver, you might be engaged in sight-seeing. The Christian journey has no accommodation for "sightseers". All passengers are called upon to be engaged, reading the signs, "wrong turn", "no U-turn", "slippery roads ahead" – to name a few; and to ensure that we follow them to safely reach our destination. God's love is given freely and in abundance. You don't have to continue on the wrong path. Trust Him today. Accept Him today.

Let us *earnestly contend for the faith which was once delivered unto the saints* (Jude 1:3) Contend means to "fight for", to "challenge for", or to "vie for". All these meanings are verbs, which suggest that we are always actively participating, "*contending for the faith*", on this highway. Again, there is no place for sightseers on this throughway.

Life

A journey much travelled
Memories heavy or light
Carried with joy or tears
Armored with daily strength
Though sometimes puny and tired
Life with its sorrows and joys
Anchored with unwavering strength
A journey travelled by all

Maps, compasses, books and bags
Now fully prepared for journey and all
Yes, fully prepared, or so you thought!
Rough roads, green paths, parched lands
Rocky plains, valleys; hills and mountains to climb
Beauty and Splendor, Disappointments and Fears
All intermingled – to make a beautiful life

A journey with its pros and cons
A journey travelled by all
Hated at times, revered at others
Travel this journey not alone
A winding road, a rocky path
A helping hand sometimes
That is the journey called life
Enjoy it all and live it well

THE CHRISTIAN'S JOURNEY # III

Rest if You Must

Scripture Meditation
Isaiah 40:29-31
He giveth power to the faint; and to them
that have no might he increaseth strength.
Even the youths shall faint and be weary,
and the young men shall utterly fall:
But they that wait upon the Lord shall renew
their strength; they shall mount up with
wings as eagles; they shall run, and not be
weary; and they shall walk, and not faint.

There are times when Christians become weary and burdened down with the heavy luggage they carry on the journey. They are tempted to exit off the highway or stop at a Rest Area or Service Station for refueling, food and relaxation. Rest if you must; refuel if you must; have some food if you must! But always remember that these are temporary stops and you must get back on the path, as you must complete your journey. Different people rest or refuel at different times; we all need those moments. *Come unto me, all ye that labour and are heavy laden, and I will give you rest* (Matt. 11:28). It is in that Rest Area where God *leads you beside still waters.* It is here that he "turns you aside to be tested and tried", but it is also where "he restores your soul". You should endeavor not to stay in the rest area too long. If you do, you will not get to your destination. Also remember, rest is NOT an exit. IT IS ONLY A REST stop.

While you are resting, wait for your RENEWAL. Remember he gives power to your fainting heart. He is the one who is able to increase your strength when you are weak and to lift you up. Continue to trust and *wait* upon God. He shall give you new strength every day. You shall *mount up with wings as eagles; they (you) shall run, and not be weary; and they (you) shall walk, and not faint* (Isa. 40:29-31).

Are you at the rest area today? You've had your time of rest and restoration. Now it is time to get back on the journey, fully renewed and rejuvenated for the next leg of your travels. Time to GO again. You now have the GREEN light. You are ready to continue with the hope, the grace and the peace that God alone gives. Always remember, He will renew your strength for the journey. Keep travelling on. Follow the signs that are leading home: KEEP RIGHT. Get back in the one-way lane; for that is the way that leads to our heavenly home! Remember, *being confident of this very thing, that he which hath begun a good work in you will perform it until the day of Jesus Christ* (Phil. 1:6).

OUR ROCK # 1

Anchored in Christ Our Lord

Scripture Meditation
Deutoronomy 32:4
*He is the Rock, his work is perfect: for all
his ways are judgment: a God of truth and
without iniquity, just and right is he.*

Psalms 18:1-2
*I love you, O LORD, my strength. The LORD
is my rock, my fortress and my deliverer; my
God is my rock, in whom I take refuge*

In the Old Testament the Messiah is often referred to as a Rock. So in the New Testament, Paul, as well as Peter, understood that passages like Isaiah 8:14 and 28:16 referred to Jesus the Messiah. Jesus himself understood that he was the rock. In Matthew 21:42, He quoted Psalms 118:22 in reference to himself, "*The stone the builders rejected has become the capstone; the LORD has done this and it is marvelous in our eyes*"

Jews from the beginning prophesied of the Messiah, Jesus Christ, as a rock, lying in the way of the Jews, the people of God. He came and talked to them, taught them, proclaimed the kingdom of God to them, performed miracles for them, and rebuked them for their evil deeds. They ignored this Rock, confronting them, therefore, they faltered and failed.

There are only two responses to Jesus Christ, our mighty Rock. We can rest on Him, believe on Him and be saved, receiving salvation by grace through faith in Him; or we can kick against Him and be destroyed, and be eternally lost. This is emphasized in the words, *wherefore Because they sought it not by faith, but as it were by the works of the law. For they stumbled at that stumblingstone; As it is written, Behold, I lay in Sion a stumblingstone and rock of offence: and whosoever believeth on him shall not be ashamed* (Rom. 9:32-33). Here Paul presents us with a stone: "a stone that causes men to stumble and a rock that makes them fall."

Let us for a moment look at the attributes of this Rock, Jesus Christ:

He is the **Immovable Rock** - cannot be moved. *On that day, when all the nations of the earth are gathered against her, I will make Jerusalem an immovable rock for all the nations. All who try to move it will injure themselves* (Zech. 12:3). This is a picture of the church built and anchored upon the foundation of the Living Stone, the Messiah. He shall not be moved!!!

Our Lord is the **unchangeable Rock**. *Every good gift and every perfect gift is from above, and cometh down from the Father of lights, with whom is no variableness, neither shadow of turning* (James 1:17). *Jesus Christ is the same yesterday and today and forever* (Heb. 13:8). He remains the same for ever and ever!

He is our **Rock of Salvation**. According to Isiah 28:16 He is our "sure foundation", a "tried stone", a "precious corner stone". In order to be saved, we must put our trust in the Rock, the Messiah. We can lean totally on this trusted rock and be safe or we can trust in our own filthy self-righteousness and ultimately suffer everlasting punishment. Religion, philosophy, science or our learnedness will not save us. Only our true faith and trust in the Rock can do that.

This stone laid in Zion is a massive, strong, consistent, unchanging, abiding, reliable stone. It is a tested stone. It is Jesus Christ the true rock of all ages.

Christ is the foundation stone. He is the sure foundation for the church. Jesus says to Peter, *And I say also unto thee, That thou art Peter, and upon this rock I will build my church; and the gates of hell shall not prevail against it* (Matt. 16:18). No one can destroy the church because no one can destroy this foundation stone, Jesus Christ. This foundation shall never give way; regardless of hail, floods, storm, and rain or any other turbulence. Our Rock is mightier than anything the devil can marshal against God's people. The gates of hades shall crumble before the church that is built on this foundation.

Let us not build on the sandy foundation of human philosophies and ideologies. This "sand" foundation of human righteousness must be rejected. It is, in essence, "filthy rags". Let us build on the Rock, our Messiah. Build on the foundation of grace and righteousness; live by faith in Christ, our foundation stone.

This Rock breaks the rebellious, the arrogant, the unyielding, and the unbelieving. God offers to us his free, gracious salvation to be received by faith. If we do not receive it, He will break us.

How will you respond to this Rock? *This is the stone which was set at nought of you builders, which is become the head of the corner. Neither is there salvation in any other: for there is none other name under heaven given among men, whereby we must be saved* (Acts 4:11-12). This rock is the Son of God, the Messiah, the only Savior. If you have not yet confessed this Rock as your Saviour, the Holy Spirit says come! Let us all humble ourselves, and repent of our sins, believe on the Lord Jesus Christ, and be saved today. Then you can say like the psalmist, *I will love thee, O Lord, my strength. The Lord is my rock, and my fortress, and my deliverer; my God, my strength, in whom I will trust; my buckler, and the horn of my salvation, and my high tower. I will call upon the Lord, who is worthy to be praised: so shall I be saved from mine enemies.* (Ps. 18:1-3).

This stumbling stone is a massive stone, not a pebble. This stone is a living person, the Lord Jesus Christ. He is our Messiah, our Stone, our Savior and Lord. Anyone who rests on, and is anchored in this rock, by believing in Him and committing himself or herself to Him, will enjoy everlasting peace and eternal life

OUR ROCK # II

Our Confidence in God's strength to Save Us

Scripture Meditation
Psalms 18: 1-3
*The Lord is my rock, and my fortress, and
my deliverer; my God, my strength, in whom
I will trust; my buckler, and the horn of
my salvation, and my high tower. I will call
upon the Lord, who is worthy to be praised:
so shall I be saved from mine enemies.*

Psalms 18 was written by David when the LORD saved him from his
enemies, including Saul. The analogies used are very representative
of the places in which Christians sometimes find themselves.

David who had had numerous experiences and encounters with
God, sometimes found himself in a lowly estate. Here he talks about
God as his protector, and gives a long discourse on what his enemies
sought to do, but with his trust in God, he ultimately overcomes. It
is a triumphant declaration made in a season of great victory. It is
true that David *decided* to love the LORD; but even more true is that
he simply felt *compelled* to love the LORD who had delivered him so
wonderfully. He makes this proclamation using very strong words
or phrases. *The LORD is my rock, and my fortress, and my deliverer;
my God, my strength, in whom I will trust; my buckler, and the horn
of my salvation, and my high tower* (Ps. 18:2).

David saw God as his **Strength**, the One who empowered him to survive against his enemies. He called Him his Rock. Here he likely meant it in more than one sense. A rock was of help to the ancient Judean in several ways. It could provide essential shade, always needed in the merciless sun and heat of the desert (Isa. 32:2). It could provide shelter and protection in its cracks and crevasses (Exod. 33:22 and Prov. 30:26). The rock could also provide a firm place to stand and fight, *as opposed to sinking sand* (Ps. 40:2).

The Christian is assured of safety and security in God's unmovable strength. We stand firmly and securely in that strength! We can *run and hide in his shadow* (Isa. 49:2).

David hid from his enemies in woods and fields. He hid behind rocks and on the top of hills. He was assured of one thing. Where ever he ran, God would be there as His Rock and Protector. God was his **Fortress,** a place of strength and safety, a place of refuge where the enemy could not penetrate.

As our **Deliverer,** God is the one who makes the way of escape for us when we feel trapped by life's circumstances. He frees us from the traps of the enemies and delivers us from the pitfalls they set for us. Our God is "My *strong God*". He is not only the object of our adoration, but He is our strength in weakness. He is also our **Buckler,** a type of shield that comes between us and the harm the enemy devises for us. So yes! We can rest assured on our Rock!

In this very appropriate metaphor in Psalms 18, God is the *Horn of my salvation*. This shows the confidence David had in God's ability to defend and save him. We should be filled with the same confidence today, as God has not changed.

As David with great confidence and assurance heaped honour on God, we should be doing the same with assurance in His person and ability. He was David's ultimate safety, and He is ours too. We can call upon God in every situation, *In my distress I called upon the LORD, and cried unto my God: he heard my voice out of his temple, and my cry came before him, even into his ears* (Ps. 18:6).

He remains our *High tower,* in a high place among the rocks, safe from plunder and destruction. Our high tower is a place from which we can see our enemies coming before they are able to attack us. We should always remember that God is all of this to us - our *God, rock, fortress, deliverer, strength, buckler, horn of our salvation, and our high tower.* We, therefore, should *call upon the Lord,* and so we will be saved from our enemies. (Ps. 18:3).

THE FAMILY # I

Harmony in the Home

Scripture Meditation
Romans 12:16-18; 1Peter 3:8; Col. 3:12-13

Over the years as we raised a family, it was not always smooth sailing or even peaceful at times. There were times when sister and big brother were in contention, brother and brother not so much as they were 9 years apart (of course until they got older), and of course we parents and our children were naturally at odds in many circumstances! There was the time when a brother asked his sister to borrow her car. She refused to allow him to use it. So he slashed her tires!!! Note, it was during those rebellious teenage years when, as a mother, I really thought I was going to lose that son (who will remain nameless here). He was just on a totally rebellious path, and that is why it amazes me now to see the wonderful, calm, caring young man he has become. Thank God for prayer and fasting!!!

Then there was the time when my daughter, speaking to her dad, and being angry at me, referred to me as, "your wife" (instead of "mom"). He was extremely enraged, as he thought she was being disrespectful to me, so he gave her a good spanking!

Oh and there was the time when dad was spanking one of the boys (who will tell you he got the most spanking – "beating" as Jamaicans would say), and his sister felt that her dad was going too far, and verbally intervened. I don't have to tell you how big that became! Dad then left the house, drove around for about an hour, returned, called the family together and debriefed the whole situation and, yes, apologized for his excessiveness. That simple action went beyond measure in healing our family at the time!

We live in a world today where families are being torn apart. Spouses against each other, parents against children, children against parents, siblings against siblings; and it seems everyone is getting at the other.

The devil realizes that if he can weaken the family, the battle is half won, because if the family is weak, our church is weak and our society is weak!

In order for the family unit to function efficiently, every member of the family must know his/her role and perform it well. Once we start performing the role of others, conflict will occur.

Love and respect for each other are the overarching characteristics that must be practiced in the home by all members of the family. Extremely crucial is the love and respect that is manifested between the father and the mother. They set the tone in the home.

In Colossians 3:18 wives are reminded to *submit yourselves unto your own husbands, as it is fit in the Lord.* Then we are admonished, *Husbands, love your wives, even as Christ also loved the church, and gave himself for it* (Eph 5:25).

Imagine the happy home when husbands start **loving** their wives as God loves the church and when wives start **submitting** to their husbands and being their biggest supporter. Imagine the positive impact on the children in the home!

As parents we have many responsibilities to our children. In effect, the Bible admonishes us not to provoke our children, *And, ye fathers, provoke not your children to wrath: but bring them up in the nurture and admonition of the Lord* (Eph. 6:4). Having said that, we are expected to instruct our children well; and are reminded of the importance and virtue of *one that ruleth well his own house, having his children in subjection with all gravity* (I Tim. 3:4). Even though this reference is to the office of a Bishop, every Christian parent, (especially fathers) is called upon to rule his/her home with diligence; understanding that, good or bad, we have great influence over our children, *He also walked in the ways of the house of Ahab: for his mother was his counsellor to do wickedly* (II Chron. 22:3); conversely, we recognize Lois' and Eunice's good influence over Timothy (2 Tim. 1:5).

As parents we have the ability to counsel our children to do good or evil; to choose to live uprightly or wantonly. We can choose to model positive or negative influences. Remember, we can only counsel, model and pray. The rest is up to our children.

No one ever said it was easy to be a child, a parent, husband or a wife. Except the Bible, there are no other adequate manuals for any of these roles. It takes full time commitment; **YES** commitment. God honours our commitment in this covenant relationship. While there is so much disintegration in the institution of marriage and so many marriages and families are falling apart, we must trust God completely and unequivocally to keep our marriages and families intact. As parents, our responsibility is to endeavor to remain blameless before God when it comes to the physical, emotional and spiritual nurturing of our children; and to prepare them to become positive world citizens, while fully looking forward to the eternal home and the hope that we have in Christ Jesus.

Again, consider this: When marriages break, the family unit disintegrates and later that spills directly into our churches and the broader society. Let us hold fast to this great institution of marriage and consistently and arduously work to strengthen our marriages. Being human, it is quite understandable that there will be failures and defects in our familial relationships. This, however, does not alter the importance of building and sustaining a healthy family relation. Spousal and parental relationships are bounded by unity and love. It is my prayer that husbands, wives and children will place much emphasis on their roles in their God-given relationship and aim to please God in all their ways.

THE FAMILY # II

The Caring Husband: The Loving Priest & Father

Scripture Meditation
Gen. 2:23-24; Duet. 24:5; Eph. 5

My friends always joke that my husband "spoils"me. To be honest, I really do not understand what they mean, except that I think because he loves and cares for me in very practical ways, they call it "spoil". On his way home from a trip to the city, he ensures that he finds a shop which sells something that I really like (as simple as a D&G pineapple soda – Jamaicans will know this), and he brings home a treat for me. If I am upstairs watching television, sitting in a really relaxed position and don't want to disturb that but I need the remote which is in the same room but a little way off; I will call him from downstairs and ask him to give me the remote. He will just look at me with disbelief, roll his eyes, and with a smile, hands me the remote; and before he leaves the room he will say, "do you want anything else?" My answer would be "no" but within minutes he would be back in the room with a cold or hot drink on a tray, depending on the weather. When my sister Sheila visits, if my husband happens to be leaving the house he would say to her, "take care of Patsie". Her quick response would be, "A she must tek care a mi, a she a mi big sista an a mi a di visita" (translation- She is the one who should take care of me; she is my bigger sister and I am also the visitor) No, contrary to popular belief, he doesn't spoil me, he loves me!

It would also mean he has spoilt his children too; as he has always made a conscious effort to see to their every need. Our daughter bought a house and went to live on her own at age 29. The first thing her dad did was to call the security company and get a security system installed. He made sure that his name and number were on the system. The joke was, every time my daughter left home he would literally know. She liked to go to Walmart late at nights, so he would be calling her every now and then to find out why she was going out so late, and giving her a good lecture on safety. She finally found a way to avoid that! Unknown to him she would turn off the security so he would not be able to track her moves. Hah, needless to say when he found out what she did, he was not very happy. For years he would call her every night to find out if the doors were locked and if the security system was on; to the point that when the call came each night, before he said a word she would say, "yes dad, yes dad", in response to those two questions. Then there were the times when he would just randomly drive 25 minutes to her home, check the front door to make sure it was locked, then return home without her knowing he was ever there. Now the boys, both adults, live on their own, and every now and then I hear the calls and the conversations, "Where are you? Did you eat? You can come and get dinner, drive carefully", and the counsel goes on! Are we "spoilt"? No! Just a husband and father who loves and cares for his own!

Of course I will not tell you about the long family worship sessions when everyone was falling asleep because he chose to read the longest scripture passages, asked every member of the family to comment on a verse of his or her choice, then literally "preached" on the passage himself. Thank God for my husband, the father of our children!

A father's love is strong, supportive, kind, everlasting – a type of God's love. The prodigal son says, *I will arise and go to my father, and will say unto him, Father, I have sinned against heaven, and before thee, And am no more worthy to be called thy son: make me as one of thy hired servants.* He then *arose, and came to his father. But when he was yet a great way off, his father saw him, and had compassion, and ran, and fell on his neck, and kissed him* (Luke 15:18-20).

This story emphasizes the forgiveness and compassion of a father. Though the child has transgressed, in compassion, the father reaches out to forgive. This serves as a great pattern for us today. Fathers are called upon to correct, forgive and embrace their children in love. This is the type of unconditional love that God extends to us.

Not only is the husband called upon to love and care for his children, but as the loving Priest, he is also called upon to love his wife *"as God loves the church"*. He is the head of the home, and as such, he must maintain his God-given responsibility of facilitating the spiritual growth of his family, while also providing for their temporal needs. Love, protection and interest in his wife's welfare are paramount to his leadership in the home. His wife must feel "covered" by him at all times. Honour, appreciation, understanding and thoughtfulness, along with absolute faithfulness in marriage are required from the godly husband. His children also must feel protected in his love; and always have the understanding that while he will not condone, they will always have his love and support.

The husband is called upon to love his wife. This puts a check on authoritarian, self-serving, insensitive leadership in the home. The duty of husbands is to love their wives. The love of Christ to the church is an example, which is sincere, pure, and constant, notwithstanding her failures.

THE FAMILY # III

The Wife: Submitting to Her Husband

Scripture Meditation
Ephesians 5; Proverbs 31; Colossians. 3:18-19

As a youth growing up I was very argumentative. I had to have the last word! As I got into marriage and realized that I had married a man who also had to have the last word (even though to all outside of the home he seems so "easy", so "calm", so "quiet - can't mash an ant" –a Jamaican saying). Of course I immediately saw that if our marriage was going to last, someone had to give. Since I was brought up being told the woman must be submissive to her husband, I took that literally and fought less for my "position" or my "rights". Many men take that literally also, and I still can remember in our early marriage my husband used to say, "A mi a di man in dis house" (I am the man in this house), when he felt like I was being overbearing. As the years went by, we both realized that submitting does not mean that the wife has to be subservient or that the husband has to be domineering, but among many other things, it means that the wife must be a helpmate to her husband and he should be the spiritual head or leader that God has called him to be. Once we understood our roles, life got somewhat easier, and the quarrels became much less frequent. What an amazing journey we have been on!

In the worldly sense, the word "submission" has a negative connotation. In the Christian world, however, when we think of the word "submission" other words like "humility" "gentleness" "patience" and "respect" become eminent. Wives yield in love to their husbands' responsibility of leadership. Wives must develop the God-given task of helping, loving, respecting, and assisting their husbands. Purity, submissiveness and a quiet gentle spirit are paramount in fulfilling the biblical call for submission of the wife.

Being submissive does not mean being weak. Importantly, we are to follow the Lord Jesus who, although He was Lord, showed humility as He took a towel and basin, and performed the lowly servant's task of washing the disciples' feet (John 13:1-17). Being submissive also does not mean that one is always fighting for one's rights, demanding equal treatment. *A submissive person trusts God to meet his or her needs.* He or she does not have anything to prove. A submissive person is not argumentative, aggressive, brash, obstinate, and hard to get along with. Instead, the submissive wife grows in humility, gentleness, patience, forbearance, and love (Eph. 4:2). Her life is under the control of the Holy Spirit, who produces joy and gratitude.

A godly woman actively submits to her husband; choosing to put herself under his leadership, and choosing to be obedient to God and her husband in the marital relationship. A wife shows submission unto her husband when she allows him to take leadership in the relationship. His position as leader is biblical (1 Cor. 11:3). Note carefully, women are not instructed to submit to their husbands because we are expecting them to be kind, tender or caring (Eph. 5:22). "A woman therefore does not submit because her husband deserves it in his own merit; she submits because she knows it is pleasing God. There will be times when a woman needs to submit, and her husband does not deserve it from a human perspective. But by divine right, God set the man as leader and a woman can trust that God is good" (Carm.org).

THE FAMILY # IV

Serving As a Godly Wife

Scripture Meditation
Ephesians 5:22-24
*Wives, submit yourselves unto your own husbands,
as unto the Lord. For the husband is the head of
the wife, even as Christ is the head of the church:
and he is the saviour of the body. Therefore
as the church is subject unto Christ, so let the
wives be to their own husbands in everything.*

Genesis 2:24, *Therefore shall a man leave his father and his mother,
and shall cleave unto his wife: and they shall be one flesh,* illustrates
the law of "leaving" and "cleaving". Once married, the primary
relationship is with your spouse! There continues to be important
relationships and space for others in your life, but according to the
bible this marriage relationship must take priority. The couple must
"cleave" to each other. The Merriam dictionary defines the word
"cleave" as "sticking closely" together; another defines it as "to adhere
firmly and closely or loyally and unwaveringly". This definition
certainly sums up the relationship within the marital bond.

It is important that a woman marries her friend, then it becomes
easy to serve. A godly wife should be her husband's most ardent
cheerleader, supporter, and confidant. A woman serves her husband
when she nurtures and nourishes the relationship (your thoughts - *so*

what happens to the men? Of course it goes both ways but I'm now speaking to women about how to serve as godly wives)

A godly wife is called to serve and stay focus as she fulfills her roles. What are some of these roles?
A godly wife needs *to honour and esteem the needs of her husband* ABOVE her own (*I hear groaning!*). Yes, this is a contentious issue, but it is all about the law of sowing and reaping. As we place the needs of our spouse above our own, we nurture our one-flesh relationship. Regardless of response, we continue to sow, eventually we'll reap (*contentious again*)!

A godly wife serves as her husband's strongest supporter (Eph. 5:22 –24); I Pet. 3:1-2). Men have an instinctive desire to conquer. Supportive wives give them the courage to step out, while criticism keeps them from going forth boldly, actualizing their full potential.

Godly wives are also called upon to respect the authority God has placed in their husbands as the head of the household. Yes husbands and wives must work together at decision making, but godly wives submit to their husbands, understanding that they continually pray for God's direction to lead. Thus being in agreement in prayer, the godly wife allows God to direct. Being in agreement does not mean icy silence, leaving it up to him, waiting to see him fail. It certainly means agreeing in heart and spirit, praying in earnest and at times compromising.

God has created an order which includes a masculine 'headship'; not *of authority but of responsibility and loving care* (John Stott). "Where love and mutual respect rule the home, there will be little problem with submission on the part of the wife...The husband is not a dictator, but he exercises his headship primarily by service. This is the same way that Jesus expressed his headship over the church" (Bruce Stewart).

THE FAMILY # V

Children in the Family Relationship

Scripture Meditation
Deuteronomy 5:16
*Honour thy father and thy mother, as the LORD
thy God hath commanded thee; that thy days may
be prolonged, and that it may go well with thee,
in the land which the LORD thy God giveth thee.*

Eph. 6:1-2
*Children, obey your parents in
the Lord: for this is right.
Honour thy father and mother; which is
the first commandment with promise.*

*I recall many mornings as a child when we were awakened to
participate in family worship. We would lie in bed and listen to the
songs, pull the cover over our heads and roll over with disgust as
"they" were disturbing our sleep! Of course, reluctantly and after many
attempts by our grandparents and our mother, we would literally
"drag" ourselves into the prayer room. I even remember, after getting
older, calculatingly suggesting to my mom and grandparents that we
should have family worship on Saturday evenings; knowing that a).
it was easier for me to miss it, and b). I could sleep in my bed on a
Sunday morning undisturbed! Of course that didn't work! At that time
I didn't fully grasp the importance of engaging in prayer as a family.
Years later, having the pleasure of being a parent, I reminisced on and*

cherished those memories, as they now inspired my husband and me to lead our family in worship.

Paul reminds Timothy *that from a child thou hast known the holy scriptures, which are able to make thee wise unto salvation through faith which is in Christ Jesus* (2 Tim. 3:15). Timothy's mother invested in teaching him the word and interacting with him. Time spent interacting positively with our children is invaluable. Teaching them to pray, read their bibles and live a lifestyle that is pleasing to God from a young age is priceless.

The world is in chaos because there is confusion of roles in the families. It is crucial that parents and children build a relationship so that interaction is easy. It seems, however, that in an effort to build these relationships some parents have missed the mark, and have ultimately caused more harm than good. Parents wanting to please children, wanting to be their buddies, have relinquished their role as parents. Children, in many instances have become rude and insubordinate and have totally missed that God asked them to respect and honor their parents (Eph. 6:1-3). That is the *first* commandment with promise!

It is time for us to teach our children to return to God and to urge them to practice God's precepts. Many parents have children who have strayed from the guidelines and principles taught to them; and at times this causes discouragement and frustration for Christian parents. It is Satan's ploy to allow us to doubt God. We will not fall for his wiles. He is the enemy of our souls. Our families need to cry out to God in repentance and return to Him in "sackcloth and ashes". Keep praying and trusting God; the seeds that were planted will grow into full bloom.

Once the family unit is strengthened, our churches, and ultimately the broader society will be strengthened. I encourage all to place emphasis on drawing your family in the presence of the Lord. It is in the family circle that the first messages are preached through our words and deeds. Your children will call you "blessed" for teaching them the way of the Lord.

A GODLY MOTHER IN AN UNGODLY WORLD # I

Godly mothers are women of sincere faith

Scripture Meditation
2 Timothy 1:5
When I call to remembrance the unfeigned
faith that is in thee, which dwelt first
in thy grandmother Lois, and thy mother
Eunice; and I am persuaded that in thee also.

My daughter chooses her greeting cards very carefully, so when I got this bookmark in a birthday card from her two years ago, I felt truly blessed. "A strong woman is one who gives selflessly, and loves wholeheartedly. She is not afraid to be bold. A strong woman is courageous. She is able to hope when things look hopeless. A strong woman in her essence is a gift to all the world – A strong woman like you" (agc.llc).

It is often said, "Behind every great man is his mother". Mothers do influence their sons and daughters! One of life's greatest blessings is to have a godly mother, thus, one of the greatest gifts you can give your child is to be a godly mother.

Timothy's grandmother, Lois and his mother Eunice, had a profound Christian influence on him. We learn that the sincere faith of these women allowed them to instruct Timothy from his earliest days. Their example and the results in Timothy's life show us that through faith in God, and by honoring His Word, godly mothers have great influence as they train their children.

While God intends for the father to take the lead in the spiritual training of the children, the mother can have a great influence, even in situations where the father is passive or hostile to God.

A godly woman needs "sincere faith". The word "sincere" means, literally, not hypocritical, being honest and genuine. This does not imply perfection, but it does imply having genuine understanding of who God is. It means that she sincerely believes in Jesus Christ as her Savior and Lord and is unequivocally able to share Christ to her children at all cost. It involves a daily walk with Christ, spending time in His Word and in prayer, thus measuring her daily walk with His word. When a mother does that, she is able to resist sin against her children, and when she errs, is able to ask their forgiveness and seek to work on her weaknesses.

Having "sincere faith" means a mother is able to develop godly character qualities and attitudes, and is willing to submit daily to God as she spreads His joy and love for her children and for mankind at large. A godly mother's children will realize that, while she is not perfect, she walks and lives in God's presence.

As godly mothers of sincere faith, we must seek to pass on that faith to our children. Our children will emulate the genuine faith they witness as we live in sincerity and unity with Christ. If we live pretentious lives, our children will read it like a book and will want no part of that pretentious lifestyle and our "Christianity".

Genuine faith is infectious. Just as we see Timothy exhibiting the sincere faith of his grandmother and mother, if we are genuine in our faith and trust in God, our children will cultivate the same faith in God. Let us pray that our daily lives will always be a true and living example of the sincere faith that God calls us to have in Him; and by so doing, our children can pattern our lives.

A GODLY MOTHER IN AN UNGODLY WORLD # II

Godly mothers honor God's Word and train their children to live by God's Word

Scripture Meditation
2 Timothy 3:16-17
All scripture is given by inspiration of God, and is profitable for doctrine, for reproof, for correction, for instruction in righteousness: That the man of God may be perfect, thoroughly furnished unto all good works.

God's Word is mighty to save, and is sufficient to sustain us throughout our lives and in every situation. How do we communicate the importance of God's word to our children so that they will come to a true understanding of the powerful implications of His word?

God's word is profitable for teaching us the ways of God and how God wants us to live. Our cited scripture reminds us of the multi-faceted purposes of God's word in our lives. Godly mothers, therefore, will communicate to their children that the word of God reveals the very thoughts and purposes of their hearts. *The word of God is quick, and powerful, and sharper than any two-edged sword, piercing even to the dividing asunder of soul and spirit, and of the joints and marrow, and is a discerner of the thoughts and intents of the heart* (Heb. 4:12).

The word reproves us; which means, it persuades us of our wrongs. It corrects us by showing us how to turn from sin to holiness and righteousness. It trains us in uprightness, showing us how to keep on the path of submission to God's way while basking in His love and blessing.

The word of God is given to be profitable in regards to how we live; to correct us and keep us on God's path of holiness and righteousness. Our children should see us applying the scriptures in our daily lives. We should also teach them how to apply them to the things they face as they grow into maturity. We should use God's Word to lead our children to the saving faith and knowledge of our Lord and savior. Mothers will say as much as they can to their children, but until they walk with them through the word of God they are not equipping them to live godly in this ungodly world!

The main way our children will grow up to love and serve God is through His Word. God's Word of truth is powerful to save. John 17:17 says, *sanctify them through thy truth: thy word is truth*. The best thing we can do for our children is to instill in them from an early age the importance of reading, studying, remembering, obeying and living God's Word.

As a godly mother grows in her love for God's Word; so will her children. If her children rarely see her seeking God through His Word, they will be little inclined to do so themselves. When they see her changed through her increasing understanding of, and conformity to the Word, they will be motivated to study the Word for themselves.

Pray with and for your children. Read the Bible with them. Encourage them to read the bible and pray even when you are away from them. Only by doing these things can you successfully train your children in the ways of God, in this ungodly world.

A GODLY MOTHER IN AN UNGODLY WORLD # III

Godly mothers have great influence on their children.

Scripture Meditation
Psalms 127:3-5
Lo, children are an heritage of the Lord:
and the fruit of the womb is his reward.
As arrows are in the hand of a mighty man; so are
children of the youth. Happy is the man that hath
his quiver full of them: they shall not be ashamed,
but they shall speak with the enemies in the gate.

As a high school teacher for many years in the Toronto District School Board, I saw all types of mothers! There was the mother who would come to Parent Night who was so strict that she would slap the child across the face, right there in the interview, if she got a bad report about her child. Then there was the mother who thought her child was an angel and did nothing wrong. Another mother who sat in the interview and allowed her child to be disrespectful to both her and me. Yet there were those mothers who anyone could tell from the interactions with their children that they had good relationships, the children knew their boundaries and respected their mothers, and the mothers respected their children. There were mothers who blamed the school for everything that was going wrong for their children, and those who saw the school as the primary source of their children's discipline. Needless to say, after every Parent Night I would walk into my classroom the next morning with a new perspective about each *student, and many times had to pray in earnest not to allow the events of the previous night to have a negative influence on my interactions with my students.*

Of course the school has an important part to play in the training of our children. Yes, we also rely on godly Sunday School teachers, youth workers, elders, pastors, or other men and women of God to positively influence our children. It is important to note, however, that the strongest influence anyone can have on a child is the influence of a mother; thus we need to pray sincerely for godly mothers to stand firm in this ungodly world

Godly mothers need to plant godly seeds and trust God for their growth.

> *Never could it be possible for any man to estimate what he owes to a godly mother. Certainly I have not the powers of speech with which to set forth my valuation of the choice blessing which the Lord bestowed on me in making me the son of one who prayed for me, and prayed with me. How can I ever forget her tearful eye when she warned me to escape from the wrath to come . . . How can I ever forget when she bowed her knee, and with her arms about my neck, prayed, 'Oh, that my son might live before Thee! (Spurgeon)*

Paul reminds us to speak *the things which become sound doctrine . . . The aged women likewise, that they be in behaviour as becometh holiness . . .That they may teach the young women to be sober, to love their husbands, to love their children* (Titus 2:1-2).

Godly mothers must love and care for their children, but most importantly they must instill a Christian worldview and lifestyle in them. Because mothers have a great influence on their children, "saying it" is not enough; teaching them through the mother's own lifestyles is invaluable.

It is imperative that mothers care for the spiritual, emotional, and physical needs of their children. In so doing they are fulfilling God's mandate to them as parents and they are also preparing their children for their quest as parents. Psalms 127:3-5 reminds us, *children are an heritage of the LORD: and the fruit of the womb is his reward. As arrows are in the hand of a mighty man; so are children of the youth. Happy is the man that hath his quiver full of them: they shall not be ashamed, but they shall speak with the enemies in the gate.* Godly mothers should see it as their duty to develop Christian character in their children, teaching them the art of self-control and purity.

No one said a mother must be perfect, but she must take seriously the sacred role that God has given to her and aim to seek God's face to be the godly mother He has called her to be. Mothering is the toughest assignment handed down to women. A mother plays the role of psychologist, drill instructor, nurse, negotiator, teacher, banker, friend, comforter, and nurturer - just to name a few, among all the other roles she must fill. Despite all that, being a mother is the most meaningful role in a woman's life.

Understandably, at times many mothers feel like they have failed in their role. It is in those moments that they need to turn back to God and walk with Him in earnest faith so that they can lead their children and grandchildren the way God wants them to.

"When all is said, it is the mother, and the mother only, who is a better citizen than the soldier who fights for his country. . . She is more important, by far, than the successful statesman, or businessman, or artist, or scientist" (Roosevelt).

WHAT IS YOUR OFFERING?

Scripture Meditation
Leviticus 1; Psalm 145; Deuteronomy 12:6

In Leviticus chapter 1, the Israelites were instructed to live their lives through spiritual and moral purity; and encouraged to separate themselves from the evil ways of other nations and live in obedience to God. When they sinned, they had to offer sacrifices of ox, rams goats, turtle doves etc. to God through the Priest, as an atonement for their sins

Today, we are not called upon to give ceremonial sacrifices, but to give our bodies, as a holy, living, and acceptable sacrifice, and to offer especially the sacrifices of a broken heart; for through this, our person and service become acceptable to God.

One offering we can give to God is that of Self Sacrifice. This is a difficult offering. By offering up ourselves wholly to God, we declare that we worship Him only. We commit to give God the first fruit of our time and service. This comes with the desire to make the sacrifice - Sunday morning service, Sunday School, Prayer Meeting, Bible Study, and the list goes on! Our commitment and service is not just about attending all these meetings. These are helpful, but more importantly, is the time we sacrifice in studying and meditating on the word. Interestingly, we tend to make time and sacrifice ourselves (time and resources) for many other things in our lives; but sacrificing for God's business becomes difficult. Let us consider getting to the place where we stop putting God's business on the "back burner", waiting for what is left to give to Him, literally the crumbs! How about making a commitment today to give God first – whether it is your service or your talents or (even) your money! He will do the increase if we give these offerings to Him from a pure heart.

What are we sacrificing? God is telling us that He has had enough of our empty burnt sacrifices. Yes, He must get the first fruit of our labour whether it be in money or time and substance, then and only then will the blessings flow.

God is calling for a recommitment to His will and His purpose. He is calling for people who are ready to sell out to him substantively in word and deed. He is calling for a different kind of sacrifice - sacrifice of the heart

- What is my offering to God Today?
- What am I holding back from God which should be an offering to Him?
- How much more can I offer to God through praise, worship and thanksgiving; and sacrificing of time and resources?
- Are my offerings going up to God as a sweet smelling savour?
- Is God pleased with my Offerings

SPIRITUAL RENEWAL

Scripture Meditation
2 Chronicles 14

Spiritual Renewal is the process for growth and transformation into the image of God. In our daily lives we strive to enter into God's presence, and strive to become united with Him by grace. God created us in His image and after His likeness. We strive to be like God.

And Asa did that which was good and right in the eyes of the LORD his God: For he took away the altars of the strange gods, and the high places, and brake down the images, and cut down the groves: And commanded Judah to seek the LORD God of their fathers, and to do the law and the commandment. Also he took away out of all the cities of Judah the high places and the images: and the kingdom was quiet before him (2 Chr. 14:2-5).

For Spiritual Renewal to take place, Asa *did that which was good and right in the eyes of the LORD his God.* Even though he lived in a time of idolatry when true worship of God declined and various places of idolatry were created, when Asa became King, he set out to purge idolatry, and urged Judah to return to God Almighty. He demolished the altars of strange gods and commanded Judah to seek the Lord God of their father and do His law (2 Chr.14:4).

Seeking God is essential to any renewal or revival among God's people. "Seeking" means, to desire and pursue earnestly the Lord's presence and His Holiness. It involves turning to the Lord with one's whole heart, and remaining in fervent prayer. It involves hungering

and thirsting. *Then shall ye call upon me, and ye shall go and pray unto me, and I will hearken unto you.*
And ye shall seek me, and find me, when ye shall search for me with all your heart (Jer. 29:12-13). Seeking the Lord for renewal means that we are confident that He *is a rewarder of them that diligently seek him* (Heb. 11: 6).

Let us consider our own lives. In order for Spiritual Renewal to happen, we need to break down the walls in our lives. We need to tear down the idols in our hearts and seek God.

During the first month of any year, especially, believers seek and make pledges for spiritual renewal. This, however, should be our continuous prayer and not only at special times of the year. Consider today your day of rebuilding and renewal and pledge to make every other day just that.

Asa rested on God for renewal. Tearing down, removing and rebuilding are essential factors in renewal. What is it that God is admonishing you to tear down today in order to renew your relationship with Him? God gave Asa and his armies victory after a time of renewal and recommitment. God calls to you today for renewal. Let us begin to remove and tear down, and earnestly pursue God and seek to rebuild our altars; and we will be amazed at what God will do in our lives.

RECOGNIZING AND DEALING WITH HURTS & HUMILIATION

Scripture Meditation
Luke 4:18
*The Spirit of the Lord is upon me, because he hath
anointed me to preach the gospel to the poor; he
hath sent me to heal the brokenhearted, to preach
deliverance to the captives, and recovering of sight
to the blind, to set at liberty them that are bruised*

Many times in my personal life I have had to deal with hurts. This I think is not unique to me as we are all human, flawed ourselves, and living in a world with flawed people. The hurts that pain most are those that come from people to whom we are closely related, whether our family members or those in the Christian community. It is truly painful when the hurts come from people who you really love and care for and people you trust wholeheartedly. Many of us will honestly say we have had these experiences, with varying degrees, and if you are like me, have spent many sleepless nights worrying and wondering why? Of course, some of the answers have still not been given, but truly God has led me to a place where I can learn to accept and move on with heart-felt peace. I am cognizant of the fact that as much as others might have caused me pain, in my humanness, I must have also caused pain to others, even unknowingly. My daily prayer is that God will create a spirit of forgiveness in my heart and in the hearts of those against whom I have inadvertently erred. God is faithful!

We live in a world where, at varying times and to varying degrees, people have been insulted, had their ego bruised, experienced hurt, felt powerless, diminished in some way, humiliated and unfairly treated. *The word "humiliate", means to cause (a person) a painful loss of pride, self-respect, or dignity* (dictionary.com); and comes from a Latin word, *"humilis", which means, low, lowly, (from humus), ground; literally, "reducing to dirt"* (https://www.wordsense.eu/)

When any of these happen, one is left feeling angry, sad, and defeated, and possibly goes on a quest for revenge. In recognizing hurt, one must know the signs: feeling disrespected, loss of stature or image (usually an image change reflecting a decrease in what others believe about your stature). If you have experienced an event in which you perceived you lost honor, and experienced shame, felt powerless, ridiculed, and scorned, and experienced contempt at the hands of others, then you may feel truly hurt and with good reason. Repeated hurt and pain can and will lead to a fragile self-esteem. While humility is considered a strength, humiliation is hurtful. Shame is private, humiliation is public. A person who willfully causes hurt is usually all or any combinations of, extremely negative, nasty, miserable, whiny, jealous, inconsiderate, selfish, mentally ill, judgmental, egotistic and surprisingly, hurting.

People experience hurt in various relationships: marriage, parental, friendships, familial, employment, and the list goes on. In most cases there are three involved parties:

a) the perpetrator exercising power; b) the victim who is shown powerless and therefore humiliated; and sometimes, c) the witness or observers to the event.

There are some hurts, wounds and pain that remain long after the events that caused them; hurts that have not healed and therefore disrupt people's lives. Such hurts are sometimes referred to as "scars", but that is an inappropriate term. A scar indicates healing of a wound. Unhealed hurts are open wounds that continue to fester and flare up, causing emotional pain and suffering.

Sometimes hurting people also become manipulative, and treat people like objects, rather than people. Sometimes threats or abuse including, verbal (e.g. name calling), physical, psychological, or sexual are part of the manifestations of a hurting person. A person who is hurting can suffer a wide range of consequences. These include, but are not limited to: low self-esteem, social isolation, academic failure, underachievement, marital conflict, delinquency, abuse, depression, learned helplessness, social disruption and many other negative consequences, even death.

While the good hearted person wants to help, he or she must be aware that there are some things that are beyond his or her scope of expertise and try to get the hurting person appropriate, and possibly professional help, depending on the depth of the hurt. Toxic people cause hurt in the lives of other people and even in one's desire to help, one can be hurt in the process. A toxic person can be a family member, spouse, friend, associate, workmate, boss, anyone, and someone that is very close to you.

Many people have carried hurt, pain and anger for years. Many have engaged in persistent and unregenerated sin in their lives. Many are bruised all over, emotionally and spiritually. To continue to harbor those hurts and pains will only cause more hurt. Be purposeful in the effort and desire to move forward; as continuing in that state means you are moving farther and farther away from the nature of God.

As we go through life, it is inevitable that we will go through various hurtful experiences. If unfounded, simply ignore them (don't take the bait). Be brave enough to describe why it is unfair and don't be afraid to ask your offender for an apology. Whether he or she apologizes or not, do not be stuck in the rut and pain of the hurt. Set boundaries and take charge. Toxic people can drain your health, energy, well-being and sanity. Until you stop allowing a toxic person to hurt you, he/she will continue to do so. Moving on can sometimes be difficult but one must purpose in one's heart to move forward. Whatever the situation, do not be afraid to solicit external or professional help. God's blessings will not flow in our lives until there is soundness. If you have been hurt, it is time to bind up the wounds and forgive. If you have caused hurt, ask for and pray for forgiveness. If others refuse to forgive, there is little you can do. Move on. The ointment of the Holy Spirit is remarkable at binding wounds. That is why Jesus came! Let us open our hearts for the outpouring of the Holy Spirit and see the amazing healing that God will accomplish in our lives.

WAITING PATIENTLY

Scripture Meditation
Psalm 40:1
*I waited patiently for the Lord; and he
inclined unto me, and heard my cry*

Psalm 37:7
*Rest in the Lord, and wait patiently for
him: fret not thyself because of him who
prospereth in his way, because of the man
who bringeth wicked devices to pass.*

*My sister Sheila has always admonished me on the virtue of patience.
I would go to pick her up for an appointment and sit in the car huffing
and puffing because I told her I was on my way and when I got to her
house she would still not be outside waiting. Of course, anyone who
knows her, knows she was putting on the finishing touches of her make
up! Then she would come out and I would say, "Sheila even though
I told you I was on my way I still had to come to wait!'. Her calm
response would be, "Patience Sis. patience."*

*For the past 29 years, every summer trip that my husband and I have
taken has been with a friend who we will call Bess. On one of our trips
to Miami we decided to go shopping. We entered this one store. After
nearly two hours with my husband waiting for us outside, the store
proprietor went to console him, "Sir, you are the most patient man in
the world! You deserve a medal for waiting on these ladies for such a
long time!"*

Alas! My husband was not so patient when we went to Panama and spent a whole day in one mall, and still needed to shop more, then the next day Bess and I asked him to accompany us to the same mall to complete our shopping. Needless to say, he "put his foot down" (translation – firmly decided) and refused to go, choosing instead a relaxing day at the hotel. Just a note: everyone who knows us understands that my friend is totally responsible for these long shopping trips, definitely not me! I only accompany her as a "patient" good friend should!

Just think of the patience that God has with us. We become wayward at times yet He patiently waits for us to return to Him. In our natural self, many times we become impatient with God. It is said that we live in a "microwave" age where we want everything NOW. *Lord, teach us to wait on your way, wait on your will, and wait on your time.* The period of waiting on God is not always easy. It may involve many tears and pain, but we are assured that He will always come through for us. People will give advice that looks and seems well. They will tell you what you should do and what they would do in similar circumstances. If you are not praying and trusting God you will be tempted to "drive off", just like I was tempted many times when I had to wait on my sister. Stay firm, it may look long but God will always show up for you. You may lose patience and decide not to "go back to the mall the next day", but probably it was just then that the best sale was on! When we lose patience with God, it is just the time when our blessing is near. Don't ever give up. Be persistent. God supersedes all persons and all elements in our lives.

Waiting is two-fold. We are encouraged to wait on God when we ask Him to accomplish things in our lives. Being patient while we wait is paramount. We wait without murmuring or complaining. We wait without sinking in disillusionment. This will only happen if we remain in meditating and reading the word; and in constant prayer for patience.

There is also another type of waiting. Daily, God waits for sinners. As you read this today you might not yet have had a personal encounter with the Lord. He is waiting patiently for you. My dear husband waited for my friend and me shopping in one store for 2 hours! Can you imagine how long God has been waiting for you? Days, weeks, months and years! He is saying, it is time, *all that the Father giveth me shall come to me; and him that cometh to me I will in no wise cast out* (John 6:37).

RETURNING TO GOD
IN SINCERITY

Scripture Meditation
Isaiah 1:1-20

The name Isaiah means, "The Lord saves" and he is commonly known as "the prophet of salvation". Isaiah confronted the nation of Israel and other contemporary nations with the word of the Lord concerning their sin and God's coming judgment. He then prophesied hope to the Jewish exiles that would be restored. He also prophesied that God would send a Davidic messiah whose salvation would encompass all the nations of the earth. Isaiah predicted that the coming Messiah would enable righteousness to shine brightly and salvation would be eminent for all who would receive it. In most of the first 39 chapters of the Book of Isaiah, however, Isaiah warns and denounces Judah for its idolatry, immorality, and social injustices.

Both Israel and Judah had turned from God and His laws and had turned to heathen nations and their false gods to deliver them from their enemies. Isaiah warned that they would be destroyed because of their sin and apostasy. Israel had fallen into a state where they *had high views of the scriptures but failed to abide by them.*

Oh what a place to be! As you examine yourself, is that where you are today? Are you in a backslidden state? It is in this context that the first Chapter of Isaiah is introduced.

Isaiah was commissioned by God to go forth without fear or doubt; he was to go under the anointing and with a Holy mandate to give the message from God. *Hear, O heavens, and give ear, O earth: for the LORD hath spoken, I have nourished and brought up children, and they have rebelled against me* (Isa. 1:2).

Judah and Israel had received God's law. He had cared for them, provided manna for them, provided water in the wilderness, given the Ten Commandments, and provided good leadership in Moses and Aaron. In their rebellion and state of apostasy, it was time for God to remind Israel of all the things He had done for them. In like manner, He reminds us today of all that He has accomplished in our lives, yet we continually turn from Him.

Hear, O heavens, and give ear, O earth –Listen carefully! He called upon them to listen, just as He is calling upon us today. We have had many encounters with God. He has given us many promises, has taken us out of many situations but we have turned from Him and have disobeyed His laws and his precepts. We have lived sinful lives and have not acknowledged God the way we should. We have not acknowledged Him as the source of our blessings; consequently, He will send judgment upon us.

Many of us, like the Israelites, have become wonton and wayward; we lie, we steal, we backbite, and do all manner of abominable things in God's sight. We have become murmuring and insatiable. Believe it or not, people who murmur and complain, and speak with ill will towards others, are the ones who cry that God is not blessing them; they just do not understand that they are plundering their own blessings by the life they live and their failure to abide by God's law.

Isaiah calls out *Ah sinful nation, a people laden with iniquity, a seed of evildoers, children that are corrupters: they have forsaken the LORD, they have provoked the Holy One of Israel unto anger, they are gone away backward* (Isa. 1:4).

The term *Holy One of Israel* emphasizes the character and nature of God - His holiness. Thus, if we are to serve Him we must do so in holiness and righteousness. We must enter into a covenant relationship with Him. God's people must be holy, as he reminds us, For *I am the Lord your God: ye shall therefore sanctify yourselves, and ye shall be holy; for I am holy* (Lev. 11:44).

In an effort to bring Judah to repentance, God allowed their lands to be plundered. The people's sin had cut them off from God's blessing and protection. Persistent sin will always bring God's judgment on us.

Our homes and churches are desolate; our cities and country are desolate. We need to turn from persistent sin and return to God in repentance. Unrepentant sin will cause us to be at enmity with God. His nature is Holy so in order for us to come before Him we must be Holy. Let us turn from our evil ways and engage in giving God more praise; then we will be amazed to see how God's blessing starts to flow. In order to have the nature of God, we must move away from a state of spiritual paralysis. We must return to God in earnestness.

MAN'S FALL - GOD'S PROVISION

Scripture Meditation
Genesis 3

God had given direct instructions to Adam and Eve with regards to how they should conduct themselves in the Garden; but they refused to follow them. How many times do we find ourselves in similar situations! In Genesis 3:6, man's disobedience becomes especially evident. As Eve perceived the "goodness" of the fruit and it's "pleasantness" to the eye, she became more enthralled by it and gave little or no consideration to what God had instructed. Not only did she deceive herself about becoming wiser if she ate the fruit, but she convinced her partner Adam of this devious act, which ultimately led to man's fall. Once the fall happened (v. 7) they immediately became aware of their nakedness. Shortly after, (v.8) they began to hide from the presence of the Lord. In vv. 12 and 13, the blame game began in earnest. "She made me do it". As verses 14 through 19 show, Adam and Eve's sin of disobedience had great consequences for mankind.

Sin and flagrant disregard for God's word have devastating implications and consequences. We must listen and adhere to God's word. As a result of the disobedience of Adam and Eve, mankind fell from grace and favour with God. At some points in our lives we are all guilty of the sin of disobedience. God continually calls us to walk in unison with Him and to obey His word, yet in our disobedience, we, just like Adam and Eve, show flagrant disregard for His word. Today is a good time to examine ourselves and see how many times we blatantly reject God's word and decide how we will continue in this life.

Despite our faults and failures, and our rejection of His word, God remains faithful to us. After the Fall, He made provision for mankind to return to Him. *For God so loved the world, that he gave his only begotten Son, that whosoever believeth in him should not perish, but have everlasting life* (John 3:16).

Thank God for this redemptive act! Satan thought he had conquered in the Garden of Eden but God showed that He is unconquerable! Thank God that I am included in the plan of salvation. There is so much to be thankful for! Let us rejoice in our new bought-back freedom, and bask in the provision that He has made for our salvation. It is a gift freely given. Anyone can accept this gift at any time. If you have not yet done so, will you accept this provision of salvation – God's free gift today?

OUR HOPE IN GOD

My definition of Hope for the purposes of this meditation is, a "*firm confidence*" in future issues, based on God's promises and revelation.

Now the God of hope fill you with all joy and peace in believing, that ye may abound in hope, through the power of the Holy Ghost (Rom. 15:13). Here we are reminded of the biblical hope which fills us with joy and peace. *For our heart shall rejoice in him, because we have trusted in his holy name. Let thy mercy, O LORD, be upon us, according as we hope in thee* (Ps. 33:21-22). Here we see our confidence and hope in God. In various places in the Psalms we see where hope "maketh us not ashamed", mainly because we know in whom we hope. Hope and faith are strong anchors for believers. While we remain in a state of hopefulness, God's eyes are continually upon us (Ps. 33:18-19). Now if God's eyes are upon us, we have absolutely nothing to fear! God has proven Himself faithful and very capable.

God's word continues to be the basis of the believer's hope. Our hope must remain in God and not in our fellow human beings. God gives us grace amidst every trying circumstance that we face in our lives. When we have endured all sufferings of this earth we can remain hopeful with the knowledge that we have an ultimate in God. Our hope is eternal hope. Ponder for a moment. If you are reading this and you are without God, there is no meaningful hope. For the repented, II Corinthians 5:1-5 reminds us of the groanings we experience in the "*earthly house*", but the passage also gives us hope that we strive for our eternal home, free from all pain. What an awesome HOPE!

As we continue to hope in God, there are certain things that it behooves us to do: We must put away sinful practices and learn to live by the word of God. We should consistently seek to please God in our daily walk and strive to allow Him to get the glory in all that we do.

Our hope remains constant in Christ when we abide in Him. There is no disappointment in Him. He brings hope to the hopeless, peace to the troubled, a deep settled peace that only He can give; and He fills the heart of the mourning with joy. Let us continue to hope in the God of our salvation.

ULTIMATE JOY COMES FROM CHRIST

Scripture Meditation
Galatians 5:22
But the fruit of the Spirit is love, joy,
peace, longsuffering, gentleness, goodness,
faith Psalm Galatians 35:27
Let them shout for joy, and be glad, that
favour my righteous cause: yea, let them say
continually, Let the Lord be magnified, which
hath pleasure in the prosperity of his servant.

As a sixteen year old girl, I was filled with exceptional joy when at the Island Convention in Jamaica a young man that I secretly admired came to me and said, "I am giving you 3 years to get saved and then I am going to marry you". Of course I was a little taken aback as I had given my heart to the Lord at age 10! The truth is, however, that part of the statement was of little importance to me, I was more excited about the "coming to marry you in 3 years!" I was "walking on cloud nine" as Jamaicans would say (translation - extremely happy). My friend Cynthia M. who knew that I had had a crush on this young man was almost as excited as I was. To be honest though, after the convention I did not dwell on it. I just thought this young man was only flirting as he was known to do. Can you imagine the feeling of elation I experienced when at age 19, after coming home from my first year of Teachers' College, sitting on my verandah one evening I saw a car stopped at my gate and this young man whom I had not seen in months, maybe years, other than in passing, came out of the car; this same young man who had said he would come to marry me in 3 years!

"Mi glad bag bus" (translation: I was ecstatic!). Of course, needless to say a remarkable courtship started that day and 3 years later we were married, and have been together for 44 years and counting!

You will notice the joy I experienced in my preceding anecdote. Let us consider for a moment then the ultimate joy that we can have in Christ, well beyond anything our minds can fathom, nothing (not *even the joy of a young man telling a sixteen year old he would marry her and coming back 3 years later as he said, to do so),* comes close to the joy we have in Christ.

The incomparable joy that God gives flows from God as one aspect of the fruit of the spirit, and is experienced by us as we maintain an abiding relationship with Christ. Our joy deepens when the Spirit mediates a deep sense of God's presence. As believers, remaining in the word, loving others, obeying God's commands and separating from the world, lead us to the fullness of joy in God's presence (Ps. 16:11). Only then can the believer experience the joy of the Lord, which is our strength (Neh. 8:10) Joy has delight in the nearness of God and His redemptive power. This is an attribute (unlike worldly attributes), that cannot be destroyed by heartaches, pain and sorrow. In the midst of all that, the joy of the Lord is still our strength!!!

One's joy can only be complete in knowing Christ. Daily, people search for things that will make them happy. Many turn to unseemly things like illicit sex, drugs, and inappropriate friendships when they are seeking to find happiness. Many of these, however, contribute to negative outcomes in some people's lives. The only antidote for the pain and sadness people experience is the unadulterated love of God. Persons will only experience ultimate joy that only Christ gives when they fully commit to Him.

AND THE BRIDE WORE WHITE

Scripture Meditation
1 Corinthians 6; Genesis 2

Three years of clean courtship! Not that we were not tempted like all people in the flesh would be, but God protected us and kept us sexually pure. Every day, even many years after marriage when in conversation, my husband and I gave God thanks for his graciousness towards us during those years. Our abstinence and our desire to not have a sexual relationship out of marriage had literally nothing to do with how strong we were. Here were two young people spending a lot of time together, at times alone. The only thing that kept us was our strong commitment to God and the trust that we had in Him to keep us from "falling". Not to mention that very constant in my mind, was the thought that that action would break my dear grandmother's heart to the core, as she had so much confidence in me and my "ability" to remain sexually pure. She was "counting" on me!

God calls us to sexual and moral purity. We are reminded that our body is the temple of the Holy Ghost (1 Cor. 6:19). A portion of the Wikipedia explanation of Temple is: *A temple (from the Latin word templum) is a building reserved for religious or spiritual rituals and activities such as prayer and sacrifice.* What then does Paul mean when he refers to our "body" as the "temple of the Holy Ghost"? The obvious answer, without delving into deep theological explanation, is that *our* bodies are sacred and should be reserved for the sacred things of God, serving Him in righteousness and holiness. It goes without saying then, that thinking from a sexual perspective, our bodies should be reserved for the sexual union in marriage.

This refers back to God's plan, which places the sexual union in marriage (Gen. 2:24). Marriage was created by God and is *very good*" (Gen. 2:18-24). God observed that it was not "good" for man to be alone, so He created woman and ordained marriage. Within marriage, a *man* cleaves to his *wife* and they become one flesh; this includes the sexual union (1 Cor. 6:16).

Marriage is the only relationship in which God ordained sexual union. Yes, His word explicitly forbids sexual relationships outside marriage. We are reminded that *Marriage is honorable* and the sexual relationship (the "bed"), *undefiled* (Heb. 13:4). Fornication and adultery, sexual union ("the bed") outside of marriage, is an affront of God's law.

Jesus teaches that fornication comes from the heart and defiles a man (Mark 7:20-23). We are also reminded that those who engage in lascivious sexual living, violate the law of God and need to repent of such ways or suffer the consequences of sin (1 Cor. 6:9-11). Fornication and adultery are wrong because they constitute being "one flesh" with someone other than one's lawful spouse. In order to avoid fornication and adultery, one should satisfy one's sexual desire only with one's own wife or husband (1 Cor. 7:2-4). God expressly confirms that marriage companions must be of the opposite gender and that each may satisfy sexual desires only with his/her marital companion.

"Marriage is the authorized relationship for satisfying the need for lifetime companionship and for sexual affection. But it involves one man with one woman with a lifetime commitment. Only that relationship is honorable by God's decree" (Gospelway)

Sexual relations before or outside of marriage are wrong, no matter how much we care for the other person. Later, this can also lead to mistrustfulness, disaffection, and violence, and possibly, disease. We are reminded that relations with an immoral woman leads to bitterness, dishonor, grief and destruction of the body (Prov.

5:1-18). It behooves individuals, therefore, to practice chastity before marriage and sexual faithfulness in marriage.

It was never God's intention that people should engage in casual, recreational sexual activities. When that happens, the true beauty of sexual affection is missed. The pleasure is transient and in most cases lacking in commitment. The true beauty of sexual warmth can only be fully experienced in marriage. In a committed marriage, the sexual union becomes the ultimate expression of affection, love, and companionship. This is a relationship that should be reserved only for our lawful spouse. (*Indeed, let the bride wear white)!* Sexual affection is then enveloped in the amazingly special union of love that God intended it to be.

The way to avoid immoral conduct is by *keeping our thoughts pure* (Matt. 5:27- 28). Our endeavor should be to avoid the lustful thoughts that lead to immoral conduct (Titus 2:5). There are many scriptures that remind us that God forbids "*lascivious*" conduct ((Rom. 13:13-14; Mark 7:20-23; Gal. 5:19-21, and others). We should teach our young women that the motive of their speaking, dressing, and acting outside of marriage should not be to arouse sexual desire.

As society declines, those who aim to preserve the sanctity of marriage become fewer and fewer. Let us be reminded that our ultimate groom Jesus Christ is returning to find a pure church; symbolic of this, is our earthly groom taking us as virgins, spotless, and unblemished. Virginity loss cannot be regained. Protect and preserve it. Nothing makes people more miserable than the failure or perversion of marriage. But nothing brings a grander blessing than an affectionate marriage that patterns God's design. *Whoso findeth a wife findeth a good thing, and obtaineth favor of the Lord* (Prov.18:22). Never forget, however, that God is merciful and if you err, His hands are always outstretched to welcome you back. My encouragement to young and old alike, is to wait patiently and faithfully. Stay pure. *And the Bride will indeed wear white!*

INTEGRITY IN COURTSHIP

An open Letter - From the Heart of a Mother
to a Daughter Engaged to be Married
Sunday, March 22, 2015

Scripture Meditation
Hebrews 13:4
Marriage is honourable in all, and
the bed undefiled: but whoremongers
and adulterers God will judge.

Dearest Daughter and future son-in-law (*We will name them T & J*),

This is a "mid-term check" to see how you and J. are doing spiritually. I hope that you both are still withstanding the enemy's plan. I am sending this to encourage you to remain faithful, first to God, then to yourselves and your values, and lastly to your family and the hundreds of people who are counting on you to remain sexually pure during this courtship. I am not naïve, and I understand that you are two young people who are spending a lot of time together. The "flesh" will rise up itself, but I just want to remind you that one wrong move can lead to a lifetime of regrets and unhappiness. Please RESIST any temptation to go against the will of God. Only four months and you will have each other for a lifetime. Do not taint that which God has so ably set in motion.

One of you has to be the stronger. I do understand that each will be strong at different times but one MUST remain strong when the other is weak, and vice versa, or else before you realize it, in a moment of passion, you fall into sin. T., I have always admired your level-headedness. Just hold on, so that when you both consummate your marriage whether on your wedding night (or you might be too tired then – ha!) or thereafter, you both will have the Christian satisfaction and joy that you conducted a pure courtship and you waited for that beautiful moment. I bring to you the word of God from Hebrews 13:4, "Marriage is honourable in all, and the bed undefiled: but whoremongers and adulterers God will judge." It is ok to wait, as a matter of fact, it is more than ok, it is wonderful! Take it from someone who waited during 3 years of courtship. There is no better feeling than knowing that in this aspect you did not fail God, yourself, and the people who love you! Not to mention the feeling of respect you both have for each other knowing that though you had timeless moments when you could have succumbed, you stood strong and waited.

It is not my intention to make this a long drawn out letter. The point is well put forward I think that the motive for this letter is to uphold you and to encourage you to hold out, regardless of the temptation. It will be worth it. Most importantly, it is to remind you that you are both testifying Christians, actively involved in ministry and cannot afford to fail God – as you do not want to face the consequences if you do – and there are always consequences!

My prayer is that when the moments of temptation come (as I am sure they have and will within the next 4 months), that you hold on to your FAITH in God and your belief that He is able to spare you from this too. T., I know J. is there to visit at times. Put up your spiritual guard. The time will come for you to be endlessly open and ready – it is not yet that time. The devil is cunning. We should not give him tools with which to work. Your actions and intentions at times might be innocent, but it is in one single moment of weakness that we fall. Be on your guard against the wiles of the devil.

Daughter, I felt led to write this to you both. As I think about you and how much I love you as my only daughter, I cannot express how much from the bottom of my heart I admire, love and respect you. You have made your dad and me proud, and we just want you to continue holding up your head. God has been faithful to us.

May the grace of God be with you both, may his peace be with you and may His love continue to shine on you and abide in your hearts.

Blessings and love,
Mom

CHRIST – OUR HIGH PRIEST

Scripture Meditation
Hebrews 4:15
*For we have not an high priest which cannot be
touched with the feeling of our infirmities; but was
in all points tempted like as we are, yet without sin*

Hebrews 2:17
*Wherefore in all things it behoved him to be made
like unto his brethren, that he might be a merciful
and faithful high priest in things pertaining to God,
to make reconciliation for the sins of the people.*

Before any high priest could mediate for the people before God, he first needed a mediator himself. But Jesus fulfilled a role which no human could ever fill. Before Jesus, a high priest could only enter into the Most Holy Place once a year; and even then, the priest could not come directly into God's presence. Sacrifices had to be offered, and the incense had to be burnt. But when Jesus came, all that ended. Jesus Christ is the perfect High Priest, able to represent His people, yet not in need of redemption as we are. Christ as our high priest is able to go right to God's presence every day, to plead our case. He has done away with the external regulations which applied until the time He came with a new order. There is now no need for the blood of goats and calves for our atonement.

Christ our High Priest, is without any taint of sin or imperfection, thus, He can enter into the presence of God without the need of a sacrifice. Because He is perfect, He enters into the throne room of God every day, not just on the Day of Atonement. As our representative, Jesus went before God and asked for our atonement, and consequently, through the shedding of His blood, has achieved for us the perfect redemption and atonement, eternal redemption.

No sacrifice of goats and calves could ever effect permanent peace with God. These sacrifices were temporary and inadequate. What Christ accomplished through His redemptive blood will last forever. His atoning blood is not transient; it is eternal. There will never be a need to repeat this sacrifice; never a need for a "do over". This eternal sacrifice both covers the sin (*expiation*), and takes away God's wrath (*propitiation*).

Jesus was the perfect High Priest which could offer the perfect sacrifice, giving up His life in our place. He died that we might live. The Gospels tell us that when Jesus died the temple curtain was ripped in two, from top to bottom. That ended the separation of God from us, his creation. No longer are His people kept out of the Most Holy Place, where prior to that, the High Priest could only enter once a year. Thanks to the Sacrificial Lamb, our Lord Jesus Christ, we can enter the Most Holy Place every day!

His Blood cleanses us, and also covers our sin and our conscience. The sacrifices of the Old Testament had their purpose, though limited in effect, pointed us to the ultimate sacrifice, Christ Jesus, who frees us from all sin. We no longer need to shed blood in order to come into fellowship with God. Christ has already shed His blood. He has washed us from our sins, and has given us a perfect redemption. His ultimate sacrifice has set us free from the bondage of sin and death.

How can we respond in gratitude for this eternal sacrifice? As we have received grace from God we must come to Him in righteousness and holiness. We must also pray that He grants us the ability to extend grace to our neighbors, just as we have received grace from Him.

God is a merciful and forgiving God and even though we have rebelled against him; we at times have not obeyed Him or kept His precepts and principles according to His Word, He is still a merciful God and still has His arms outstretched to us – offering the redemptive blood through Jesus Christ our High Priest.

Our part is to come to Him in humility and repentance and ask Him to forgive us. The price for our sins has been fully paid. We can enter boldly and with confidence into the Holy Place, only because of the shed blood of Jesus. The curtain is now open. Let us *draw near with a true heart in full assurance of faith, having our hearts sprinkled from an evil conscience, and our bodies washed with pure water* (Heb. 10:22).

True Friendship

A Friend – a precious gift some say,
Laughter, tears, joys intermingled in this friendship shared
Odd betrayal at times
Confusion and disgusts at others
Yet true friendship, rocklike solid, stands

Storms, wind, water and rain
Earthquakes, tornadoes and pain
True tests of friendship be
To the powers of none, yield true friendship
It stands firm

A listening ear, a guiding word
Sometimes liked, sometimes not.
Frowns at times, but mostly smiles
Friendship long and dear, surviving the tides

Loving, giving, sharing – bouncing back!
Enjoying love, laughter, joy and true friendship dear
Powerful sweet confusion
The reality of true friendship shared!

THE BLESSED MAN

Scripture Meditation
Psalm 1

As you will note from some of the anecdotes, God blessed our lives with good friends when we came to Toronto. In 1885 my husband's father suddenly passed away. By then, we had had 2 children, I was on my last few courses at York University, still paying as an International student. My husband was the only bread winner and there was very little money to go around. About 4:00 a.m. I called my friend Sharon S. to give the news of my father-in-law's passing. She lived on the same building. She came immediately and spent the rest of the night with us. The next morning, before she left our apartment, she pulled me aside and this was what she said to me, "Patsie, I know you guys don't have any money. I don't have cash to give you, but here, take this – my credit card. Use it and buy anything you all need. Buy something nice for you and Trevor to wear to the funeral, buy anything you need to carry and use it to pay your air fare. Don't worry about paying me back now, you can do that whenever you are able." This is the same friend whose husband at the time (we affectionately called Chan - may his soul rest in peace) who co-signed with us for our first car in this country, as we had not yet built up credit to stand on our own! We felt truly blessed to have had friends like these in our lives.

What does it mean to be blessed by God? To us as humans it sometimes entails material things like I referred to in the anecdote, a beautiful house, a prestigious car, a well-paying job. All those are important and have their place; but being blessed by God goes far beyond those.

A blessed man is cleansed and controlled by the spirit of God (Rom. 8), and capable of experiencing the peace and joy of God in all circumstances (Phil. 4:6-7).

In the cited scripture, the blessed man's character is determined by how he chooses to live. The scripture gives graphic description of the contrast between the good (godly) man and the evil (sinful)) man. The GODLY is characterized by righteousness, love and obedience to God's word and separated from unrighteousness; conversely, the ungodly represents the counsel and the ways of the world, who does not abide in God's word and who is cynical to the things of God

We are blessed if we do not walk in the counsel of the ungodly (sinners); a warning to many Christians who would rather take council from sinners than brethren; do not stand in the way of sinners or do not sit in the seat of the scornful (v.1) Does that mean you must have absolutely nothing to do with the unsaved? NO, it means you must choose your associates wisely and stick with people who are able to uplift you spiritually and not pull you down to their sinful ways! Both the righteous and the sinner can be distinguished by their lifestyle and associations and the things they delight in.

No person can experience God's blessings without turning from harmful and destructive behaviors. Those who are blessed by God not only turn from evil but they build their lives among God's people and His instructions. They genuinely take pleasure in God and His beauty; and pattern their lives according to His word. Love for God and His word motivates us into good deeds (v. 2).

When we seek to live godly lives we meditate on God's laws, which in turn shapes our thinking, attitude and actions. We read the word and ponder on it. In pondering, we ask ourselves questions like: Is God's spirit applying this verse to my life? Is there a promise here for me to claim? Is this passage revealing a particular sin that I must strive to avoid? Is my spirit in harmony with what the Holy Spirit is saying? Is the passage expressing a truth about God, salvation, sin?

When we are blessed by God and following in His word we are like a tree planted and fully secured, solid and strong. The imagery of being fully secured "planted by the rivers of water" is a beautiful one for the Christian. The child of God who is planted by grace, grows continually, is full of sap, and maintains leaves that do not wither, but remain green at all times. That Christian is fruitful and always flourishing. As we draw life from God we live fruit bearing lives.

We must strive to be continually watered by the word. Our indulgence in the word should be a lifestyle. This is how we are preserved from blemish or decay. Those who delight in God and in His word are rooted in Him, draws from Him, and have their being fully secured in Him. They also experience an unfailing source of life from His Spirit. *Whatsoever he doeth shall prosper* (v.3) does not mean that the godly person will not experience life's challenges; rather it means that amidst those, that person will be upheld by the Spirit of God and will continue to abide in His will and favour.

This text paints a stark contrast to those who are "planted" and those who are like the "Chaff" blown by the wind, (vs.3& 4). As blessed people of God, we should aim to be always "planted" by that ever-flowing river. *Therefore the ungodly shall not stand in the judgment, nor sinners in the congregation of the righteous. For the* LORD *knoweth the way of the righteous: but the way of the ungodly shall perish* (vv. 5&6). This depicts the separation between these two kinds of people, the blessed Godly person and the ungodly; and suggests that this will exist throughout history and into eternity.

The Godly person who is continually planted in Christ and remains fruitful will be rewarded with a crown of righteousness, and will spend eternity with Christ. The unrepentant sinner (the ungodly) who is like the chaff blown away with the wind, will be condemned before God on the Day of Judgment. He or she will perish for eternity.

The enduring question here is, where do you see yourself and how can you make sure you are living as a blessed, godly person? Remember, being blessed is not just about a friend helping you out with her credit card in your moment of need, or co-signing a loan for you (though these are good deeds toward you). It is also not just about living in a big house, having a nice car or being employed in a well-paying job! It is more about your relationship with, and commitment to God. If you are considered blessed and serving the Lord, then continue in His path; stay rooted by *the rivers of water* and continue to flourish to bring glory and honour to God's name. If, however, you are not yet committed to Christ, and is being *"like the chaff"*, blown by the wind, it is time to consider yielding to the Holy Spirit, confessing your sins and committing to Christ. It is time to find a new path. As you yield to God He will raise you up and allow you to sit in *heavenly places in Christ Jesus* (Eph. 2:1-6).

DRAFTED TO SERVE – STAYING FOCUSED

Scripture Meditation
Psalm 100:2
Serve the LORD *with gladness: come*
before his presence with singing

As a youth leader I was honoured to "delegate" responsibilities to some of our very able youth. My "other daughter" Sophie M. named me "Delegator in Chief". I remember vividly the many occasions I called upon Trevlin and Sophie to go far beyond reasonable at times. They never frowned and even when I got annoyed at them for minor failings (which was rear as they did everything with precision and excellence), they would serve with a smile. It would be hard to find a more diligent pair in ministry. They took their draft seriously!

I am blessed to be married to a man who takes serving his wife very seriously. For many years and even now, no matter what he is doing, at a certain time every night, my husband dutifully makes me a cup of hot chocolate (or another preferred drink) and brings it upstairs to serve me.

In the early 80's after completing my qualifications to teach in Ontario, and while doing "Occasional Teaching" during the days, I worked full time at a bank as Manager for the Data Processing Department. Occasional Teaching was the route to go if I wanted to obtain a full-time teaching contract. My shift at the bank was from 6:00 p.m.-2:00 a.m. Then if I had a teaching job for the day, the call would come before 7:00 a.m. My husband was my strength. He would never wink *an eye until I came through those doors at 2:45 a.m. every day. On days when it snowed heavily, leaving the children with my dear cousin Joan (Nichols) Fearon, he would drive 45 minutes to my place of work to wait in his car so that when I was finished at 2:00 a.m. he could drive behind me to make sure I got home safely. That's a husband serving and protecting his love with an earnest heart! He took his "draft" very seriously.*

In rudimentary writing we teach children that when writing a paragraph, they should consider the 5 "W" and possibly 1 "H" (Who? What? When? Where? Why? How?) My focus will be on this same principle as we consider the thought of being "Drafted to Serve & Staying Focus". Two important "Ws" in the Christian's draft are: Who has called us? Why has He called us? The word "drafted" may seem like a strong word as it has militaristic implications. In the Christian army, however, let us consider very carefully who it is that has drafted us, why we are drafted, and how we must serve when we are drafted.

Just like in the army, when you are drafted into the body of Christ there is a call for discipline, and a willingness to fight against all circumstances in order to win the battle. There is always an urgent need to stay focused in order to achieve ultimate victory, and this is paramount in "God's Army". You must "bring the cup of chocolate" willingly and consistently, every day and every night! You must be willing to get out of your beds at 2:00 a.m. to protect others against the "snow". It might not be a drive in the wee hours of the morning, but you could serve by interceding for another soldier who is facing difficulties on the battlefield. Every Christian must see himself or herself as being an integral part of God's army. As you commit fully to Him and serve Him in earnest, He takes care of all aspects of your life.

You are called upon to serve the Lord joyfully. No matter where you are positioned and no matter what responsibilities are placed upon you, you should diligently execute with gladness, and ensure that your service brings glory and honour to God's name. You are not serving the nightly "hot chocolate" for your wife to speak highly of you, though that is well noted. You, on the other hand, are serving that the Kingdom of God will flourish and He will be pleased with your service. We are drafted to serve God and His people. Let us serve in this most prestigious army of all, joyfully, and willingly! Our medals await us!

Men o' War

Beaten, Beheaded, Blinded
Men o' war, that's your fate
The fight is on –
Will you be beaten?
Will you be beheaded?
Will you be blinded
NO! The Sword will be drawn
We'll fight to the end
Armored and ready.

Mangled, Menaced, Mistreated
Men o' war, that's who we are
The fight is on –
Will you be mangled?
Will you be menaced?
Will you be mistreated?
NO! The armor will be worn
We'll protect ourselves
Breastplate and all

Men o' war
Be ready
Keep on that armor
Shod those feet with the gospel of peace!
And having done, Be ready to fight
Oh Men o' War

TROPHIES

Scripture Meditation
1 Cor. 9; Hebrews 12:1
*Know ye not that they which run in
a race run all, but one receiveth the
prize? So run, that ye may obtain.*

*For years our two older children, Trevlin and Richard, along with
many other youth from the Eastern Ontario Region, participated
in Junior and Teen Talent competitions. They won many trophies
locally, regionally and even internationally, for first and second places,
especially in the Writing and Drama Divisions.*

*When our youngest, Scott, reached the eligible age for competition, he
insisted that he had to "keep the tradition going"; even vowing to outdo
both his siblings by winning more than either of them. I am still not
sure he achieved that goal, as the truth is, I stopped counting. Needless
to say, Scott was determined. Trophies and medals were important
to him. Those were symbols of victory to him. He won! He achieved!
Noteworthy, he is my most competitive child, though he does it very
subtly and pretends it doesn't matter if he wins. The truth is, the sheer
joy he shows when he wins a competition makes you happy for him.
It was our pride and joy to hear our children's names called at each
Trophy Ceremony. We encouraged and supported them to do well, and
we were proud when they did.*

In the secular world, athletes strive to win a race so that they can
attain their prize – most likely, a trophy or a medal. Olympians are
severely disappointed when they win a silver or a bronze medal –
nothing but gold matters. The ultimate prize!

At the onset of the Christian path we enter a race. This race differs from the secular one as there can be many winners and many trophies at the end. The most important thing we must do, is run "our" race well, without competing with anyone. In this race it does not matter how many trophies others have, or how much faster they run. Many people can and will win the "trophy" or the "medal" – eternal life, as long as we endure and stay in the race to the end. We are reminded to run well and run with patience. God gives us sustaining strength for every leg of the journey. Like in the 100 meters sprint, this pathway gets tiring at times, but luckily, it's not a sprint, it is long distance, a marathon. We rest when we get tired, we get up when we fall and we persevere to the end, as we know a crown awaits us (2 Tim. 4:8). There are even times when we drop the "baton", but God gives us the strength to pick it up and continue in the race, and guess what, even then, our trophy or medal still awaits us at the end.

Let us run to win so that we can receive our trophy, our reward. In this race we are not competing to get more trophies than our older brother or sister. We are in a race for eternal life. In order to win, we run successfully laying aside all the baggage that weighs us down - envy, malice, strife, backbiting and any other sin. As in running a natural race one gets tired in the spiritual race. Heartaches, pain, afflictions and distress are some of the things we will encounter in this race, but we are encouraged to run with patience and persistence (Heb. 12:1). Our "trophy", eternal life with Christ, awaits.

WHOM HE LOVES, HE CHASTENS

Scripture Meditation
Proverbs 13:24
*He that spareth his rod hateth his son: but he
that loveth him chasteneth him betimes.)*

*I am reflecting today on the many spankings, as a child, I received
from my mother and more so from my uncle Sammy who was always
the father figure in my life. Frankly, there were times when I thought
they didn't love me at all – too many "beatings", as they are called in
Jamaica where I grew up. Many years after, I literally thanked them
for those spankings, even though I jokingly tell them in today's world
they would be charged for child abuse. Certainly not! They wanted to
see us (myself and my two siblings) go in the right path. I thank God
for allowing them to be diligent in the way they brought us up.*

*As we raised our children, my husband and I, on various occasions
employed the rod. One of our children will say he got more than the
others. He knew we loved him dearly, but he was "mouthier" than the
others and challenged us more, thus more spanking. Today he jokes with
his dad about the many spanking, but they are closer now than ever; and
when he talks about his dad, he talks about him with utmost love and
respect. He still reminds his dad, however, of the time when he had a
friend (we will call him Glen) over and this son made some fries and ate it
without offering any to Glen. My husband spanked our son and told him
he should learn to treat visitors well. The funny part is, our son's friend
sat and laughed and then said, "and di funny ting is mi never want any
a di fries you know" (translation: that's really funny since I didn't want
any of the fries). Our children have never doubted our love for them. No
matter how many spankings they got, they always felt secure in our love.*

Christians sometimes need to be chastised as we do at times stray from the presence of God. Our chastening will not be physical as my mom and uncle did to us or as my husband did to our children, but we do need to be chastened by the word of God, and by leaders and fellow-Christians that God has placed in our path. It is out of love for our souls that these godly loved- ones try to see that we go on the right track. No chastening feels good when it is being given, but it usually is for the good of the chastened.

Our response to chastisement will definitely dictate our growth or lack thereof in this Christian path. Our son accepted his chastening and has grown into a young man of whom we are today very proud. When we accept chastisement in humility and bow in penitence before God, He forgives us and enfolds us in His loving care. My uncle could just be finished spanking me, but within minutes he would be hugging me. He had made his point but that did not take away the love he had for me; and I was always assured of his love. The love that God has for us, His Children, is infinite. He loves us with an everlasting love, and as such, when He chastises us we should go to Him and ask Him to forgive us of our sins. We should not pout or fight. Sometimes when God sends a word of chastisement for us, our inclination is to fight the messenger. Beware of our attitude! If a message comes, pray for God to clarify it to our heart and give us an honest open heart to receive it and grow from it. We will certainly know when a message comes from the Lord for us if we are living in His presence. God in his infiniteness loves us unconditionally. He will consistently send chastisement whether it be through a word or a song or a person. When He does, I pray that He gives us the wisdom to accept it as it is sent – in love. When we accept our chastisement we are on our path to repentance.

If you are in a situation today where you are being chastised, accept it as God's unconditional, unwavering love for you. Do not spurn it. Accept and change to the path in which God is leading you through His chastising. Remember those whom he loves, he chastens!

SECTION B

INTIMATE PERSONAL REFLECTIONS & THANKSGIVING

The anchor holds
Though the ship is battered
The anchor holds
Though the sails are torn

The Anchor Holds!

My Mother's Love

(dedicated to my mother Lucille L. Nichols-Manning)

Mothers are a gift from God.
They know your pains, they enjoy your success,
They live for you.

Thank God for the blessing of a mother who cares
A single mother with boundless pains and joys!
Raising three - at times *"tormented"*, rebellious girls!
Working tirelessly to provide for our every need

A Godly mother you have been – industriously providing for all
Truly beautiful is the way you provide for others
Always lending a hand, meeting a need
You mothered many, created a haven for many more

In moments of deep frustration, your love has always shone through
Your ardent effort to protect and care, has never gone unnoticed
Though I did not always understand your love or pain
My heart is always thankful that you are there and that you care

For allaying my fears when they were great . . .
For believing in me, despite self-doubts – I thank you

Oh boundless love!
This mother's love
Transcending love!
My mother's Love

Today and every day,
I pause to applaud you, mother,
Loud CHEERS to you I send!
As you have cheered us all along
Always in our corner - my mother is always standing firm

Mother – endeavoring always to meet our physical needs
Taking care of your household

My mother A Proverbs 31:27 mother
She looketh well to the ways of her household,
and eateth not the bread of idleness

Your diligence was and still is a shining light
You were always the wheel that allowed our home to spin
I pause to say thanks
Today your children call you blessed
Thanks for showing us the way to Christ
Teaching us there is no better way

Mother
YOU have my loudest applause
You have earned it all too well
You have my unbounded affection
And my thanks in abundance!
My dearest Mother, Lucille L.

Portrait of my Grandmother . . . a heritage to keep!
(dedicated to my late grandmother: Beryl Nichols)

She walked with elegance and grace
A woman with unmatched warmth for any race
My role model and my mentor
She was life's precious gift to me - forever!

This was my Grandmother
Soothing my sister's childhood toothaches
Calming my fears when I was worried and felt alone
Making me laugh with her unconventional vocabulary
Like: Orrett being *"Unconfidentable"*
Laughing, even when I felt like crying
My grandmother! She knew just how to make things right.

Then the days she wanted to call Lucille to *"come tek her pickney"*
That's after I had a fight at school and parents came complaining
She roared and quarreled but love shone through
"If a til u married and gone to u yard, u a get this beating!"
(Even when you are married and have your own home
You will get this spanking)
A thousand times, were those words spoken,
But even as they came, love oozed with them
Needless to say, I married, had children of my own,
But those spankings never came!

Mum, you are to me "what a woman should be"
Your tender-heartedness, your arm extended
To everyone through our gates did come
A drink for them was sure,
Those boys: Mike, Junior, Ray and Lyle, all knew"
And proud of it they were, for Mum said,
"We must get a drink whenever we come"
A good role model of kindness firm

You showed me the way that leads to Christ
Building my spiritual, emotional, physical strength were your delight

MY GRANDMOTHER
Words are inadequate – to say how much I still love you Mum
So very precious you were to me.
Thank you for your love even when unearned! Thank you for your care
Thank you for being my friend . . .
Your kind words - always smoothing my aching heart
Thank you for loving me unconditionally.
For being there, always to give an ear or to lend a shoulder.
I have loved and will forever love you more than words can tell.
No pen's bold ink can write how dear you were to me
Tears still flow when I read those precious missives you so timely penned

You gave me laughter, you gave me joy, you gave me love
And a lifetime of pleasant memories
Um, you will always be my super-hero
Mum, I thank God daily for having placed you in my life

A WONDERFUL MAN:
MY HUSBAND – ENDURING LOVE

Meditation
Mark 10:7
*For this cause shall a man leave his father
and mother, and cleave to his wife.*

Proverbs 18:22
He that findeth a wife, findeth a good thing.

I can truly add, "*he that findeth a husband, findeth a joyful life*".

Through the various anecdotes you have read bits and pieces about this wonderful man who walked into my life at age 16. It was July 9, 1977, after we had courted for 3 years that I marched down the aisle to meet the love of my life waiting for me at the altar. Thank God for that day. Our exchange of vows was the sealing of our enduring love. It was the beginning of our new life, new relationship, coming from two different worlds. Our singleness was over and forever two became one, walking "hand in hand", with God being our ultimate source. My husband Trevor has been the strength of my life. There is not a day when I do not give God thanks for him. He has fathered our three children, Trevlin, Richard and Scott, but more than all, he has been a godly husband to me. His support goes beyond measure. At our 25th Anniversary Celebration we reasserted our love for each other and pledged to remain in each other's care. As I walked down the aisle to renew our vows, I mentally played the video of the last 25 years and could not find enough praises to give to God for His faithfulness to us.

The years have had many struggles, but truly the joys have far out-weighed the struggles; and having Trevor, my dearest friend by my side has made the struggles seem much less severe. He is not always my "friend"; as at times when I am mad about something or at someone and expect him to be mad at them too, and encourage me to stay mad; he looks at me with that look, "Ok, just leave that alone". Or the times when I am ranting about someone who has offended me and expect to hear him say something, and he says NOTHING at all! Hate it! But it has been good for me. His reaction has always given me moments for sober reflection.

In my quiet moments I reminisce on different things about our lives. I think of the two young people coming to Toronto in their twenties, with absolutely no other family members. I think of the night he wrote the note as he left my sardine and rice dinner on the stove and went to his evening job, *"Your dinner is on the stove. We might not have a lot, but we have love"*. I also ponder on the many snowy nights (mentioned earlier) when he would drive for forty-five minutes to my work place at the bank, sit in his car and wait for me to finish work at 2:00 a.m. so that he could drive behind me on the snowy road, to make sure I got home safely. So many more thoughtful deeds I could list, but the picture is clear. God has blessed me with a magnificent man to call my husband.

At the celebration of our 40th Wedding Anniversary, I felt truly blessed that God had kept us together for those years. Our friends and family joined us in celebration of that joyous occasion.

I feel truly honoured to be my husband's partner in Ministry. We both knew God had the call of God upon his life, and though he resisted for many years, there came a time when he could run no more. Today he is Bishop Trevor Brown, the Senior Pastor of Temple of Praise Church of God in Toronto. Despite his diligence, with the demands of ministry, at odd times I have found it necessary to remind him that he is not only my Pastor, but he is my husband and my lover!

Today, I acknowledge and salute you my dearest Trev as the love of my life, the joy of my heart, the best father my children could call dad, my dearest friend, the priest of our home and the king of my palace!

A GLIMPSE INTO THE HEART OF OUR 3 CHILDREN – OUR GREAT BLESSINGS

Children are our gifts from God. We must bless and not
curse them. We must lead them in the will of God. Their
rebellion should not deter us in our persistence to lead
them to God through teaching of the word, praying for and
with them, and placing them in godly environment.
It begins in the home.

*Solomon, in Proverbs 22:6, encourages us to "Train up a child
in the way he should go: and when he is old, he will not depart
from it". It is our responsibility to train them in the way of the
Lord. In Deuteronomy 6:7 we are reminded, "And thou shalt
teach them diligently unto thy children, and shalt talk of them
when thou sittest in thine house, and when thou walkest by the
way, and when thou liest down, and when thou risest up."*

As parents it is our fervent responsibility to teach our children the way
of the Lord and to give them the correct instruction that they need
to live a devout Christian life. By being good examples of Christian
conduct, putting our children above professions, social status and
even church ministry, we will cultivate in them a love for God and
mankind. Fathers must turn their hearts in earnest to their children,
and mothers must not neglect the love and nurturing that is essential
to the well-being of a child. Favoritism for specific child or children
has no place in a Christian home. Parents should understand that each
child is unique in his or her own way and applaud this uniqueness,
without showing bias to one child over the other.

At an early age we should dedicate our children to the Lord. Hannah provides a great example for us (1Sam. 1:27-28). From a very early age we should instill in our children the importance of living righteously before God and imbue an awareness of God's awesomeness, so that they learn to obey His word and live by His precepts. In the world we live, our children are constantly faced with all types of endevours to lead them away from God. As parents, we should depend on and use the word of God to warn them against these ungodly influences. We should help our children to understand that though they are in the world they must refrain from, and separate themselves from the ungodly things of the world. This will be taught not by lip service but by our lifestyle. Our children should be taught the importance of allowing the Holy Spirit to direct their lives and giving God full control over ever decision they make. One important message we must communicate to our children is that God loves them unconditionally and He accepts them just as they are and will mould them into who He wants them to become (Ps. 139:14).

My Children - The Sky Is the Limit

O Children!
     The sky is the limit
          A consoling thought, and God ordained it

If those who are called by His name
Will humble and pray – He'll bless them

His words

Mediocrity and Discouragement
Fighting with success and aspiration

Settle?
Of course not – the sky is the limit

Like Eagles soar high; feathers lost and regained
     Now ready for flight again
          A Valiant Champion on your side
               Conqueror of all

The greatest Conqueror of all!!!

Embrace good thoughts – true, pure, honest, just, lovely
And of good report! Live by them!
O Children, soar high, conquer odds

The sky is the limit with the Greatest Conqueror of all
Our God!

A GIFT MOST PRECIOUS –
OUR DAUGHTER IS BORN

Scripture Meditation: James 1:17
*Every good gift and every perfect gift is from above,
and cometh down from the Father of lights, with
whom is no variableness, neither shadow of turning.*

*Our Daughter – She na go no wey she a tan wid wi (Translation:"She
is not going anywhere, She is staying with us)*
When our daughter Trevlin was born my mom came 3 months later
to attend the Christening Service. She knew we had very little and
thought it would be easier for us if we didn't have to take care of
Trevlin here in Canada, with all the hustle and bustle of our fast life
and meagre means. As her departure drew near, she tactfully opened
the subject of taking Trevlin back to Jamaica to care for her there,
until we "were in a better position", she said. Of course, I was having
nothing to do with that, but it's my mother, and Jamaicans reading
this will understand, no matter how old you are you do not say no
to your mother – (back then anyway). So I politely said, "Maybe you
should talk to Trevor about that". Yeah! Pass it on. Of course, Trev and
I had already discussed that we were not sending our child anywhere,
though we knew mom would care for her with her whole heart! We
were going to care for her with the little we had. Let him tell her "No".
Mom approached Trev and this was his response. "No nurse. Trevlin
not going anywhere. If a one banana wi have di tree a wi a share y".
(Translation: "No Nurse, Trevlin is not going anywhere. Whatever we
have, no matter how small we will make it work for the three of us). I
was never more proud of my husband. Yes, we knew that mom would
take good care of our child but we were sending her nowhere. It was

hard but it was our child, our responsibility and that precious gift was ours to care and love. She stayed with her parents.

My husband and I lived in Montreal, Canada for a year while I attended Concordia University. It was the third year of our marriage and we felt it was time to start a family. Unfortunately, as soon as I became pregnant, I had a miscarriage. I watched another woman in our church as she carried her baby to term. Every Sunday she would walk into church and I would turn my head as I didn't want to see her as she carried her child and I had lost mine!

I longed for a child. Fantasies of me not being able to have a child haunted me. We prayed and we waited and then we were given the great news – I was Pregnant!

On January 12, (year omitted- as I would get killed to expose the year), my husband and I were blessed with the most precious gift – a sweet baby girl whom we named Trevlin (really ensuring that she would always "carry" a part of each of us – Trevor & Joycelin)

What a precious gift she is! I call her the "rock" of our family. She is the person who listens, gives advice and calms us down in a "heated" moment. When I am uncertain of a decision to make, Trevlin is the person I call. When I need to vent, she gives a listening ear. She is truly my friend and confidant. I can't imagine what my life would have been without this special gift, our daughter.

Trevlin looks out for everyone's well-being, in and outside of our family, and at times much to my irritation, placing her own wellbeing aside. She is a daughter that every mother wishes to have! She finds ways to make every special occasion in our family truly special, and we are truly blessed to call her daughter!

Trevlin has served the Lord since she was a child; has been engaged in youth and music ministries in the church. She continues to serve in her area of gifting. God has been faithful to her. He has blessed her with her husband Joel, a man of God who works tirelessly to ensure the needs of his family are met. They are blessed with 2 wonderful children, our grandchildren, Nathaniel and Jonathan who bring great joy to our lives. Parents are always pouring into the lives of their children; very important though, is when a child pours into a parent. I feel blessed when I get messages like the following from my daughter:

A poem (*content unedited*) **written by my daughter Trevlin in celebration of Mother's Day**

A Mother's Love

A mother is someone who cares
For your hurts and pains
Soothes them with her calm words and tender hugs
Who understands your needs and wants
Gratifies the needs
Delays the wants

She is there to listen to you share
To be your confidant, friend and guide
How many cares does a mother's heart know?
How many sorrows does she turn to gladness?
With the right words, placed in their right places
With her tender voice singing songs of comfort,
And lullabies
Oh mother, what a joy and comfort to your children
What awesome gift!

The tears she sheds
The prayers
The trips to the basketball games, the soccer games
To swimming, to music, to Parent Night
The list is endless!

Our intercessor in the mid-night hour
When all others are asleep!
She is our chauffer
A comrade
A cheerleader

She is most often our banker
The one who spins the till and money flows
She is the sunlight in our home
With her sweet smile, her tender touch and warm meals
What else is a mother?
EVERYTHING A CHILD COULD HOPE OR NEED!

This precious soul, our daughter Trevlin has brought much joy to our lives. The care and compassion she extends to all, make her a special treasure, a rare diamond. Thanks, Trevlin, for being the wonderful person you are. Thanks for being the super special daughter you are! We are truly blessed to call you daughter. Trevie, you are a rare gem and I love you with all my heart.

OUR MIRACLE! GIFT OF A FIRST SON

Scripture Meditation
Proverbs 31:28
Her children arise up, and call her blessed;
her husband also, and he praiseth her.

But God I would have killed my wonderful son that morning!

I sat in my car as my son Richard filled it with gas. We were on our way to school. I would drop him off at his High school, then continue 5 minutes down the road to my place of work, my school. I handed him the money to pay for the gas. He did, and returned to the car with my change. I stretched out my hand for it. His very rude response was – "If you wanted change you should have gone to pay for the gas yourself". (Please understand the context; it was during his turbulent, rebellious teenage years (not the awesome wonderful young man he is today)! He was my "mouthy child". As these words came out of his mouth, everything that he had done over the past week came flooding in, and everything in me said, "take the gas hose and spray him from head to feet until he is soaked with gas"! That was how angry I was! I chided him right to his school, and by the time I got to my school they had to call the ambulance, as I was having severe chest pains! Thank God it turned out to be nothing serious.

I give God thanks daily that through these rebellious years we did not give up on my darling son Richard. Now, he is literally the calmest child we have (don't test it, please). God has given us our children and we must be good stewards toward them. I am glad I did not follow my fleshly instinct and in anger drench my son with gas. That was my reaction to the moment. What a treasure my son Richard is! Our children test us at times but God always gives the grace and wisdom to do the right thing. And when we don't, as we are only human, we should own it and ask for forgiveness from our children and God, and move forward.

Our daughter was three years old and I had already had my second miscarriage – this time, an ectopic pregnancy. Shortly after, I became pregnant again but this pregnancy was also threatened. I ended up in the doctor's office and was rushed to the St. Michael's hospital in Toronto. I was given the sad news that I had lost another pregnancy and would need to do a D&C. I cried for days, "my daughter was going to be an only child, she wouldn't have the joys of sibling fights!

Days after the D&C I continued to sleep excessively. I went to visit my friend Cynthia in New York. I slept throughout the days. I convinced her and myself that it was a residual effect of the pregnancy I had lost. As weeks went by, my stomach kept getting bigger. I told myself that I was "putting on weight" because I was depressed over the miscarriage. I wore tight girdles to conceal my "fat". I was concerned that I was putting on weight so rapidly so I visited my doctor. He quickly concluded that I had a growth in my stomach and I needed to do an ultra sound. I called my mom, and my sisters crying, "The doctor says I have a growth". I sought a second physician's opinion, he concluded that I was pregnant. "I couldn't be pregnant! I had a miscarriage and was too depressed to engage in activities that people do to be pregnant!" Scared, I went to do an ultra sound the second doctor scheduled. As the technician began scanning, she asked conversationally, "Why are you here?" I answered, "One doctor thinks I have a growth and the other thinks I'm preg. . ." Before I completed the word "pregnant", she said, "You are very pregnant". I returned, "Very", what does that mean? "You are six months pregnant", she said. "No I can't be, I lost that pregnancy, and I had a D&C to complete the spontaneous abortion"! It was confirmed. I was pregnant. After three months of intense anxiety, on February 6, we gave birth to a healthy baby boy, our first son, Richard. To this day my son believes he is the survivor of the "Twin". What a joy it has been to mother our son, Richard!

After a lovely childhood he turned out to be my headache in his teenage years. There were times when I honestly thought we were going to lose him! He will tell everyone he got the most spanking from his dad! There were times when I thought I was in the middle of a warzone, when he was rude to me and merited a spanking from his dad, then his sister would get involved to protect him! He was very naturally brilliant, and sometimes used that brilliance to be "mouthy", and I always felt that nagging desire to slap him on the mouth, just where the "freshness" (as Jamaicans call it) was coming from. As a youth he gave his heart to the Lord and as he matured out of the teenage years things changed for the better, the roaring teenage years were behind us!! Thank God we survived them!

Today I have a beautiful, wonderful son that would be every parent's dream! We call, and he comes in minutes! He tends to our every need and checks in very often, just to make sure we are ok, but of course, also to stack up on groceries for his house. He prepares my special dinner on Mother's Day (*as Trevlin is now a mother herself and needs to be pampered; and Scott will barbeque but not take the task of preparing a Mother's Day meal*). He is loving and caring and I would not give up my son Richard for anything or anyone in the world. He became a father and I am extremely thrilled as I watch the caring, responsible father he is to his beautiful daughter, our granddaughter, Janae. He makes us proud every day.

A Touching piece *(content unedited)* **written by my son Richard as a teenager; delivered by him in a service during "Black History Month" . . .**

One of the most compelling truths for me is that I am born a black MAN. What does that mean? Does it mean that I am inferior to others? NO! Does it mean that I should be subservient? NO! For me it means that I am a person, a unique individual, beautifully and wonderfully made. What a great masterpiece God made when He created ME!!!

How about you? Have you wondered why you were created . . . What purpose God had in mind for you, uniquely so, thus, no other person is quite like you? The abundance of God's blessing was fully in perspective when you were formed – in His own image according to "That Good Book". So what is your purpose? Black or white, yellow or brown, we were all made to reverence God.

During a time of celebration of Black heritage, we pause to understand that black is but a colour which defines an external appearance. Metaphorically, if one is considered "evil", it is said that one is "black"; if one is considered "good", it is said that one is "white". Let us understand that it is the intricate whisperings of our heart and soul that make us who we are. Our private personal self is what defines us, since it is what is on the inside that is reflected externally.

Regardless of the colour of our hearts, the greatest consolation is that God can change the colour and make it purely what He wants it – a heart not defined by how black or how white we are, but by how pure we are internally.

Has God changed the colour of your heart?

Let us not be mesmerized by external appearances. Let us focus on the reason for our being. Live daily in worship and adoration of our creator. As we set aside time for fun, food and fellowship, let us not forget that He who has made us, craves our praises and our hearts. Let us come together as one people, regardless of colour, creed or class, and uphold the "colourless", "creedless" Kingdom of God.

My prayer for Richard (and ask it to be yours - the reader's too) is that he will return to the Lord, to serve Him in truth and righteousness. I believe the seed is planted and the conviction is there and I will continue to trust God for Richard's return to Him. Many prophecies about his path in the Kingdom of God have been made over the life of this young man and I live in hope and prayer that one day soon they will come to pass in Richard's life. Rich, you are a rare gem and I love you with all my heart.

MARCH 30TH - INCOMPARABLE JOY: OUR LAST HOORAH

Scripture Meditation
Psalm 127:3
*Lo, children are an heritage of the LORD: and
the fruit of the womb is his reward.*

*When you love someone you always want to make sure he or she is safe;
and if you are a mother you also want to know his or her whereabouts.
Scott, our youngest child, left home for University at age 17. I still
remember the day we dropped him off, packing out his clothes in his
dorm room, stacking his fridge, and yes, crying profusely when we
left him. As most mothers would, in the first few weeks I called him
literally every day. "Did you eat? Where are you now? What are you
doing? Do you have any assignment due? Did you make a calendar
for your assignments so you won't miss a deadline?" The questions
went on and on. But as expected, the calls lessened both ways over
time. I always wanted to hear from him though, and if he did not call,
a text message would do. I just needed to know he was alright. Of
course when he needed money I would certainly hear him. There were
times when University life got busy and the calls or messages would
be less frequent. The worrying mother that I am would be calling his
roommate to ask, "Is Scott ok? Can you please tell him to call home?"
Then Scott would call, "Mom, why are you calling my friend, I just
spoke with you 3 days ago!" Nah! Too long. A mother needs to hear
her son!*

As a child growing up I had always dreamed of having 3 children.
Having had so many incidences of traumatic pregnancies, I at times

thought of giving up my dreams. I was nearing a certain age and it was now or never! *"Trevor, I'm turning Hmmm soon and if I am going to have another child it has to be now"*. It didn't take long. I visited the CNE (Canadian National Exhibition), a yearly event during the last 2 weeks of summer in Toronto. I got on the ferris wheel, and immediately after the ride I became nauseous. *"It was the ride!"* I emptied all the contents of my stomach, I was sick! *But that was the effect of the ride!* Sure it was . . . a few days later the doctor confirmed that I was indeed pregnant with our 3rd child. This was our last hooray.

All four of us waited with great anticipation for the 5th member of our family. Richard told everyone he met - his teachers, his friends, anyone who would listen, that his mom was having a baby. Trevlin couldn't wait to be a big sister – and that she truly was, caring, loving, and maternal in every sense.

On March 30th, we had our 2nd son – and much to the chagrin of our first son, Scott was constantly told by people outside of our home, that we left the "best looking" for the last (*of course inside the home we knew we had 3 beautiful children*)

Scott is our wonderful reserved child. He is a loving, caring child/ young man who blobs all over my face with his hugs and kisses. He is the one I text at 3:00 a.m. to ask, "Are you sleeping?" and within minutes I get a response, "What are you doing up at this time?" He is the child who responds 2 days after a post in our What's App family group, when the other children respond in minutes! We are always trying to keep up with Scott. He is the most independent of the three and sometimes "too independent for his own good" (another Jamaican expression). Scott has a very brilliant mind and uses it very well. Sometimes it is difficult for me with my "limited knowledge" to have conversations with my 'deep thinking" son Scott. There are days when in conversation, I have to send out an SOS call for *"HELP"*, and Trevlin immediately responds, *"You are talking to*

Scott, right?" I love Scott with all my heart and he has brought so much joy to our family. Richard bothers him a lot but both he and Trevlin take very good care of their "little" brother, our "wash belly" (another Jamaican term for the last child in the family). Scott also was baptised and once served the Lord. When I tell him that he has strayed, he consistently tells me, I shouldn't judge him, and states, "you don't know the relationship I have with God". My prayer is that he will truly return into an intimate relationship with God. I do not want to be searching for Him in Heaven! As you read this writing, please send up a prayer that God will allow the seeds of righteousness that have been sown in Scott to keep on growing.

Scott wouldn't write for me to have an original piece from him, but people have written about him. A glimpse into Scott from a couple of his teachers . . .

His middle school teacher's graduation note to him reads in part . . .
Scott, it truly has been a pleasure teaching you this year. Even though you drove me insane sometimes with your lack of agenda and a pile of messy papers you called a binder, I really couldn't help but smile when you were around. You have a very special energy Scott that will serve you in the future. You are bright and creative and I have seen such kindness from you that makes me proud to be your teacher.
I want you to promise me that you will work to your full potential in High School and be the kind of adult that I know you can be in the future.

From his Grade 12 Dramatic Arts Teacher. . .

I am pleased to have the opportunity to write this letter of reference for Scott Brown. He is a very deserving candidate for this scholarship . . . I have known Scott for 4 years in my capacity as the Department Head of the Dramatic Arts at Maple High School. Scott proved to be a very important player in my classes. He is a leader and so, had the ability to set the tone. This is not an easy responsibility for a teenager to have. Leadership comes with responsibility and although Scott is still learning to command this challenge, he proves to be more than capable. . . .

Scott quickly establishes a positive rapport with staff and his peers without reservation. Scott always finds a way to make things happen. His creativity is obviously a product of his constant drive for learning and applying. Scott is very interested in the world around him and spends a lot of time contemplating and applying. I appreciate his sense of humour and social literacy.

My classroom is based on an atmosphere of positive energy and Scott contributes to the growth of that energy every day. He always displays initiative and this makes him a very successful individual. Although his drive to success is self-motivated, Scott has always found a balance when working in groups to ensure that the collective talent is maximized.

These very befitting words from Scott's teachers speak so much to who Scott is. I can tell his middle school teacher, he may have cleaned up his binder but his room is still a work in progress. He is a brilliant soul indeed and is developing into the responsible young man his teachers, and indeed, his parents know he will become! Scott, always remember the Lord IS your ONLY source and serving Him is the only way! Scottie, you are a rare gem and I love you with all my heart.

I Am Me

I might want to live in a hot steamy desert . . .

You may want to live in the cool exotic lush plains, but . . .

I'm different . . . so what!!!

You can still love me

My differences make me UNIQUE and so do yours

But you are still SPECIAL and so am I

Please understand if I cry when you would laugh or think I should

Please understand if my mountains are your little mole hills . . .

They are important to me

Please understand if my complexities are your simplicities

I am different

I am unique

So . . . PLEASE understand me! I am Me!

I am "fearfully and wonderfully made"!

I am special!

I am ME!

Sisters: May 27th & April 17th

Sisters are a blessing. Sheila and Sonia
One from the beginning, the other joining at age 9
Transitions wasn't easy for all. Fights, Tears, joys and sorrows
Make ups were always well anticipated
The bond of sisterhood though tested and
tried will always withstand the test
One sister going out on dates of her own,
The other sister waiting for me to give her every minute detail of my date
Oh how we mocked "Victor"
The name we gave to my beau at the time
For always wearing a shirt with "Victor" written all over!
Sisters are love – with all our flaws, enough to build a mountain
But love enough to cover the mountain!

An unbroken bond will always exist between us sisters
Sometimes wavering . . .
But all times confident of the love I have for each!

One who tried hard to meet my needs
Soothing my stinky feet that no one else would touch,
Doing my chores on Saturday mornings when my lazy self would not
Listening to my every talk of romance about the one I love

The other – my longest relationship yet alive
In youth, in a world of her own with all the
boys wishing she could be theirs
Sober beyond her years – yet I never failed
to take a spanking on her behalf!
Grown into a woman who has taught me one most valuable life's lesson
To be content in every situation – no matter what life throws at me

Amid the cries, the fights, and yes, sometimes harsh words interchanged,
My sisters have always been and will continue
to be precious souls in my life
They have taught me to love unconditionally.
Through our interactions

They have taught me to be open and honest, though it hurts at times
I have learnt many valuable life lessons from my sisters - two
Every person should have a sister, I often say
My two have meant so much to me in their own special ways!

O wonderful sisters, Sheila and Sonia, I thank God for you daily!

A Prayer for Permission

Lord, grant me permission to *Love*
Though all may not accept, you've told me I must
You've shown me the way
Your ONLY son, great gift of love you gave
Spat upon, ridiculed, mistreated and disdained
Yet so much love He gave!
Lord, grant me permission to *Love*

Lord, grant me permission to *Give*
Out of a heart filled with passion and joy
Though little, may it be much
As I share with others who may have less
From *bowels of compassion* - may I give and give
With no thought of remuneration
Selflessly sharing some joy as I live
Lord, grant me permission to *Give*

Lord, grant me permission to *Praise*
Don't call on rocks to raise their voices
Cause mine will peak high above theirs
Lively echoes will buzz and chime through the air
Praises from sea to sea, from sky to sky
Sounds of gratitude will I ring
As melodious praises I raise
Lord, grant me permission to *Praise*

Lord grant me permission to *Sing*
A voice charm'd with heavenly songs
No angel's voice, but one redeemed
Tuning melodies to you the Holy One!

Awesome sounds . . . ring through the heavens loud!
Wing'd with thankfulness and adoration great
Lord grant me permission to *Sing*

Totally anchored in you Lord
Please, grant me permission to *Love, Give, Praise* and *Sing*!

SPECIAL MENTIONS

From the Author. . .

I wish to acknowledge important family members who have, over many years, played integral roles in my growth and development. Thanks to my mother Lucille Nichols-Manning who has spent her life making sure we had all the necessities of life and provided for us beyond means and measure. She has also taught me, through modeling, that extending a hand to the less fortunate, is God's hand extended. Appreciation to my late magnificent grandparents Valesta & Beryl Nichols, especially my grandmother affectionately called Mum, who taught me the way of the Lord and how to give my total self to God's service. Thanks to my dearly beloved Uncle Sammy (Donald Nichols), who though he didn't "spare the rod" as he "fathered" me throughout the years, has all my love and appreciation. He is the one I call no matter the time, when I need an ear – Uncle, you are a gem. My sister Sonia Hazle, my brother-in-law Ray and nephew Peter – God's blessings be yours. Sonia thanks for supporting my endeavours and prophesying into my life. My sister Sheila Nichols (my self-acclaimed Armour Bearer), and my niece LaShea, I pray for you daily. Sheila, you have always been one of my biggest cheer leaders, and a strong source of energy and encouragement with those very appropriate bible verses for every situation. You have repeatedly asked me, "When are you writing a book?" Here it is Sis! Thanks for always believing in me. To my many friends who are too numerous to mention by name (*without getting in trouble*), and my *Temple of Praise* family, you have all impacted my life in many positive ways.

Oh how truly grateful I am for my immediate family: our awesome daughter Trevlin Stewart and her husband Joel, our amazing sons Richard and Scott Brown; along with our three precious grandchildren Janae Brown-Wright, and Nathaniel and Jonathan Stewart. There are not enough adequate words to say how much you truly mean to me. I love you all from the bottom of my heart.

Finally, I feel truly blessed to have in my life the best man God has ever created, Trevor Brown, as my life's partner for the past 44 years. What a precious gift he is! He has filled numerous roles in my life: my husband, my ardent supporter, my confidant, my pastor, my friend, and yes, not to forget, my awesome romantic partner who has continually taken me to "places" beyond my imagination! Thank you for being my husband and Priest!

IN APPRECIATION. . .

I give thanks to God for giving me this opportunity to share glimpses of my immigrant experience and glimpses into the life of the awesome family with which He has blessed me. I give honour to Him for His grace and favour. I hope as you shared in the devotional and reflectional pieces that you have been blessed and that you have gleaned even small insights as to the amazing things God can do when we put our trust in Him.

The poetry stems from my years as a high school teacher of English, and the joy I had in looking into themes and symbolism that poetry conveys. I hope the imagery, themes and symbolism in the poems conveyed to you that at all times, light conquers gloom; and there is always HOPE!

Special thanks to Marian Smile-Senior, my College batch mate and dear friend of many years, for her endorsement and for her help in editing this book. Thanks also to Rev. Donnett Thompson-Hall, renowned Gospel artist (Toronto, Canada); to Dr. Rev. George S. Peart, former Overseer of the Church of God, Eastern Canada; to my dear past student Kezia Royer-Burkett; and to Bishop Wayne Vernon, District Overseer and Lead Pastor, West Toronto Church of God for their kind endorsements.

It is my prayer that you were blessed as you journeyed through the simple narrative of this book. I concur with the famous line of my beloved late Father-in-law Bishop Richard James Brown, "To God be the glory"; and as my wonderful late grandfather Valesta Nichols would say, "Peace and Love in the name of Jesus".

The Anchor Holds!

RESOURCES

Aglow.org - Seven Hebrew Words for Praise

He Leads Me Beside Still Waters (Song), https://www.allthelyrics. com/lyrics/unknown-when_i_am_low

How we can be a Godly Mother in an Ungodly World. | Hope... johannagash.wordpress.com › how-we-can-be-a-godly

http://biblehub.com/hebrews/1-3.htm (God's Glory)

https://bible.org/seriespage/lesson-3 (Wives Submitting)

https://carm.org/what-does-it-mean-wife-submit-her-husband

https://en.wikipedia.org/wiki/Saul_Alinsky

https://holinessisgodscommand.wordpress.com/

https://library.timelesstruths.org/music/We_Have_an_Anchor/

https://www.gospelway.com/family/marriage-sexuality.php

http://www.gty.org/products/commentaryspecial (Being Filled with the Spirit)

https://www.princeofpreachers.org/quotes/charles-spurgeons-tribute-to-his-godly-mother

https://www.sermoncentral.com/sermons/how-to-be-a-godly-mother-in-an-ungodly-world

Life in the Spirit Study Bible, (King James Version), Zondervan, Grand Rapids 49530

Mother's – A Quote from Theodore Roosevelt – Writing Canvas

writingcanvas.wordpress.com

The 7 Hebrew Words for Praise in the Bible: Share.com

Wikipedia

www.christcenteredmall.com – Belt of Truth

Printed in the United States
by Baker & Taylor Publisher Services